S O C C E R

GUARDING
THE GOAL

SOCCER
GUARDING
THE GOAL

FOR YOUTH GOALKEEPERS & COACHES

Shel Brødsgaard

BLUEFIELD ❧ BOOKS

Published by
Bluefield Books
Gr. 12, C. 9, RR 1, Winlaw, B.C., Canada V0G 2J0 1-800-296-6955

Distributed by
Raincoast Books
9050 Shaughnessy Street, Vancouver, B.C., Canada V6P 6E5 604-323-7100

National Library of Canada Cataloguing in Publication

Brødsgaard, Shel
  Soccer, guarding the goal

ISBN 1-894404-12-2

1. Soccer — Goalkeeping. 2. Soccer — Coaching. I. Title.
GV943.9.G62 B76 2002   796.334'26   C2002-910702-4

Cover and interior design by Gillian Stead
Front cover photograph of goalkeeper Peter Schmeichel and Nwankwo Kanu
  courtesy of Clive Brunskill/Getty Images
Illustrations by Angela Lockerbie
All interior photos by Christopher Grabowski, except where noted

Printed in Canada

03 04 05 06 07   5 4 3 2 1

LEGEND

⚽	Ball
GK	Goalkeeper
S	Server
P	Player
B	Bullet
▲	Cone
·······	Player Movement
- - - - -	Ball Movement

In memory of my uncle,

Møgens Brødsgaard,

who taught me to see the good in all people.

Contents

Getting Started

Footwork, Flying and Focus

3 Making the Save and Starting the Attack

4 On the Spot and In the Mind

5 Putting It All Together

Foreword

Nicci Wright at the 2000 Women's Gold Cup
PHOTO © TONY QUINN/CSA

I began to play soccer 15 years ago and I am frankly amazed at how far the game has come — especially for women and girls.

I remember watching Canada's men's team play in the 1986 World Cup. I was impressed by how athletic the goalkeepers were. But they just don't compare to the athletes that are between the pipes now! Today's goalkeeper is stronger, quicker and much more involved in the game.

Goalkeeping is a unique position that demands specialized training. Goalkeepers have always been the last line of defence. Now we are also the first line of attack. Because we play a much more active role in the game, we must train accordingly. Only with the proper training and coaching will a goalkeeper be able to gain the techniques and confidence to strive for the next level. A trustful relationship between the goalkeeper and goalkeeper coach can give both the team and the goalkeeper more confidence.

I was excited when Shel asked me to write the foreword to *Guarding the Goal*. He is my mentor, goalkeeping partner and friend. He has so much soccer knowledge to share with the developing goalkeeper or coach.

You **will** benefit from Shel's expertise. Enjoy the book!

— *Nicci Wright, goalkeeper,*
Canada's National Women's team and Alviks IF of Sweden.

Shel Brødsgaard.

PHOTO © JASON STANG

Introduction

Guarding the Goal is designed for goalkeepers aged eight to 17 and their community-level coaches. It's intended to ensure a positive and rewarding experience for the goalkeeper through a training system designed solely for goalkeepers.

Exercises are presented in three levels to challenge each goalkeeper to achieve a higher level of play and to progress relative to his or her age and skill level.

Level One is for Beginner goalkeepers aged eight to 11 years old. Goalkeepers will be introduced to the basic techniques of warm-up, ready position, collapsing, receiving and ball-handling.

Level Two is for Intermediate goalkeepers aged 12 to 14 who have advanced beyond Level One. These goalkeepers will be exposed to more advanced technical elements plus a small portion of the tactical side of the game that occurs on a regulation-size soccer field. It includes age-related warm-up, diving, high balls, breakaways, positioning, footwork, decision-making and distribution.

Level Three is for Advanced goalkeepers aged 15 to 17, or adults, who have mastered Levels One and Two. The goalkeeper's task at this level is to better understand their responsibilities within a team. The focus is on the physical and tactical elements, which include decision-making, reaction saves, crossed balls, penalty shots, mental training, strength training and positioning. Practice plans are located at the end of the book.

Whatever your age or skill level, whether you're a goalkeeper or a coach, you'll need to get ready to play. That's the theme of the first chapter.

— *Shel Brødsgaard, 2003*

Craig Forrest, Canada's legendary goalkeeper, in action at the 2000 Gold Cup.

PHOTO © DALE MacMILLAN/CSA

1

Getting Started

Do you know what my favourite part of the game is?
The opportunity to play.

— Mike Singletary

INTRODUCTION

One of my favourite pre-game rituals was polishing my boots. I would polish them over and over in the days before a match, focussing on the game and my responsibilities to the team. There were times when it became an obsession, but it has always been a factor of pride. If you take care of your equipment, your equipment will take care of you.

One day when I was 13, shortly before the provincial finals, I went with two of my teammates to get our shoes shined. I had a new pair of top-of-the-line, kangaroo-skin Keegan Gold boots. The softest leather I've ever felt. I've always enjoyed the smell of a can of polish and buffed leather. And the shine. Oh, the shine! Our coach might have thought we were a bit crazy, but it helped me prepare for the game (which we won).

I still fondly remember my first pair of Gola screw-in-cleat boots. To help break them in, I wore them in the bathtub in ankle-deep water. Then I walked around the house, hoping they would mould to my feet. Well, I fell asleep that night with my new boots on and woke up in the morning with soggy toes.

To be honest, the boots should have been stuffed with newspaper and left out overnight to dry on their own. But even now, though I'm no longer seven years old, I still wear new boots into the bathtub to help shape them to my feet.

1.1 Gearing Up: Equipment

SHOES

When it comes to footwear, always come prepared for any type of weather. The turf shoe — with no cleats — is used for training inside or on artificial surfaces.

The ideal shoe for hard ground is the multi-stud or moulded boot. These shoes provide the most comfort for you and the best traction for the surface.

The ideal shoe for wet weather or soft ground is the six-stud or replaceable-cleat boot. When conditions demand, every player on the field must wear them. Goalkeepers need a good grip to avoid slipping in the goal. Your ability to stay standing can be the difference between making a save and allowing a goal.

Above: Multi-stud or moulded boot.
Below: Replaceable-cleat boot.

TIP: ❯ For replaceable-cleat boots, take time to remove each stud and place a small amount of Vaseline on the screw. That will go a long way to preventing them from stripping.
❯ Different sizes and shapes of replaceable studs come in handy when it's extremely wet or the grass is longer than usual. ❯ If you're playing in wet conditions, take time before each game, and during half-time, to clean away any mud that might have built up around the cleats. ❯ After each wet practice or game, scrub your boots while they're still wet, with water and a brush. It's always to better to clean them before the mud dries. Then stuff them with crumpled newspaper.

GLOVES

Gloves help your hands to stay warm and dry, and to get a grip on the ball. I still remember my first pair of Uhlsport goalie gloves, which I proudly wore home from the store, around the house, and to school — as well as on the field.

There are many gloves available for you to choose. The correct size means the gloves must slip on comfortably; you'll take them on and off many times. They can be a little longer than your fingers because this provides more surface to grip the ball. Latex gloves provide the best grip, but they do wear out quickly. For beginning goalkeepers, start with the basic gloves.

Take care of your gloves. Wash or rinse them when they are dirty. Dry them overnight spread out, palms up, on a towel. Never put them in the dryer — the heat can destroy them. A glove bag is useful to keep your gloves moist. Keep the palms from facing each other to prevent them from sticking together.

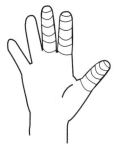

TIP: ❯ Your fingers could get sprained after stopping a lightning-fast shot from a striker, or by jamming a finger down into the ground. The easiest way to prevent sprained fingers is to take a roll of athletic tape and split it down the center. Wrap a piece of tape from the base of each finger to the tip. You should be able to bend your finger. Make sure it's not so tight that it cuts off your circulation and makes you feel numb.

TIP: ❯ Try to use an old, worn-out pair of gloves for training and a second pair, in better condition, just for games. Keep your gloves smelling fresh by shaking some baby powder inside after a practice or game.

TIP: ❯ Bring a small hand towel into the back of your net on rainy days to dry the palms of your gloves during breaks in action.

UNIFORM

A lot of goalkeepers feel better when they look good. I remember one professional goalkeeper who used to design his own jerseys — a different one for each game. There were 52 games in the season, so he had quite a collection!

Long sleeve or short sleeve jerseys depend on the weather and condition of the field. There are benefits to jerseys that have elbow pads and shoulder pads. You must decide for yourself what suits you.

Goalkeepers' shorts can provide extra protection for the hips. But, they may also feel bulky. I preferred to wear loose-fitting, non-padded shorts for games, unless I was nursing an injury. Then I didn't have a choice. Padded shorts are also helpful in training because you are diving over and over. Tight-fitting bicycle shorts are excellent to wear beneath your uniform to protect you from scrapes on the outside of your legs. Make sure to wear the same colour as your goalkeeper shorts.

Goalkeepers' pants are often padded in the knees and hips to help you cushion your fall. So, if you have sore knees from collapsing, or tender spots on the outside of your legs, make sure to wear these. They can also keep you warm in cool temperatures.

Also, take a baseball cap with you, in case you need to block the sun from your eyes.

PADS

Shin pads are a must-have. All youth goalkeepers need to wear the most comfortable shin pads that also give the most protection. Make sure to air-dry your shin pads after use. In training, some goalkeepers will also wear additional pads on their hips, knees and elbows.

WATER

The fuel that keeps you going during training or a game is water. Bring a full water bottle with you. If you're near a fountain, get a refill at halftime or during a training break. Make sure to store your bottle in the corner of your net during the game.

The Challenge of Playing Goal

On any given day, the goalkeeper can win a game with a timely save or lose it with a simple mistake or lapse of judgment.

During the 1991 Canadian Soccer League season, I was playing in a game televised coast-to-coast in Canada. Midway through the first half, a midfielder struck the ball at my goal from 22 yards out. The ball dipped between my legs and into the goal. This was the most embarrassing moment of my career.

I managed to finish the game with several incredible saves, prompting the TV commentator to mention my remarkable recovery from that terrible blunder in the first half. Learning how to recover from mistakes is an important skill.

1.2 Getting Loose: Stretching and Cooling Down

WARM-UP

Your goal in a warm-up is to raise your body heat and get ready for a workout. Skip, jog or cycle until you start to sweat a little. Then move like you do during a game or practice. Kick your knees up high or kick your butt with your heels.

Now that you're warmed up, get loose with some dynamic stretching exercises. Stretching enhances flexibility and balance. Flexibility helps increase performance and decrease the possibility of injury. Balance prevents the goalkeeper from falling to the ground, by maintaining their stance while under pressure from the opponent.

You may have some soreness at the beginning, so don't stretch too hard. Do the exercises over a distance of 20 metres. Walk back to the start position and repeat three times.

LUNGE WALK

➤ Clasp your hands behind your head and step forward. Drop into a lunge position, but keep your head up. Your back knee should almost touch the ground.

➤ Pause in the bottom position for a moment and then repeat with the opposite leg, moving forward with each step.

➤ Do the same, but try moving backwards with each step.

TWISTING LUNGE WALK

➤ Do the same as above until you drop into the lunge. Then twist your upper body so that your left elbow touches your right knee.

➤ Pause for a moment and then repeat at the opposite side. Keep your head up. Your back knee should almost touch the ground. Repeat with your left leg, touching the outside of the leg with the right elbow and the inside with the left elbow.

SIDE LUNGE

➤ Put both hands behind your head and step to the left with your left foot forward. Your foot should point in the direction you are traveling.

➤ Drop into the lunge position, keep your torso upright and you should feel a stretch in your groin. Pause for a moment at the bottom, then stand up, out of the lunge position, and bring your other leg in so that both feet are together again. Take another step with your right leg and progress so that you are going in a zigzag.

WALKING KNEE CROUCH

➤ Get into a crouch position, as deep as possible but comfortable. You should not have any knee pain. Keep your torso up. Walk the length of the course keeping your knees facing forwards and under you.

➤ Your feet are facing in the direction you are traveling, while your arms should be outside your knees and moving with the opposite knee. Your right foot moves forward at the same time as your left arm.

WALKING KNEE TUCK

➤ Step forward with your left leg and, using your hands to help you, squeeze the right knee up to your chest.

➤ Pause for a moment, then step out with your right leg and repeat the action with your left leg. Try to pull your knee slightly higher with each repetition.

TOE AND HEEL WALKING

➤ Go up on the tips of your toes and walk the length of the course You could also walk the length of the course by standing on your heels so that your toes are off the ground.

OPPOSITE HAND TO FOOT HAMSTRING STRETCH

➤ Step forward with your right foot and reach your left hand to your right foot. Your back foot can come off the ground. Stand up again. Step forward with your left foot and use your right hand to touch your left foot. Continue for the length of the course.

WALKING LEG SWING TO OPPOSITE HAND

➤ Take a step with your left leg, holding your left arm in front as a target for your other leg. Then swing your right leg up and over shoulder height to touch your left hand.

➤ Keep the leg straight during the swing and repeat with your opposite leg and hand.

➤ Try to swing slightly higher each time.

COOL-DOWN EXERCISES

Just as you warm-up before a practice or game, you should also cool-down when you're done. The cool-down helps your body slow down and return to normal after being so busy out on the field. It helps increase flexibility and prevents soreness the next day.

Just like the warm-up, you should do five minutes of light jogging or skipping. This will help relax your muscles. Next, do five to 10 minutes of static stretching. Hold each stretch for 30 seconds. The cool-down is a perfect chance to work on flexibility because the muscles are completely warmed-up and are ready to start shutting down.

Drinking some water is also part of the cool-down process. Think of cooling down as getting a head start on your next practice or game.

1.3 Strength Training Exercises

Test your strength by performing these exercises recommended by Jerry Knutsson, goalkeeping coach for Norway's Women's National team.

➤ First, place a ball between your feet and do "v-sits" — move your arms and upper body towards your legs while moving the lower half of your body up. Repeat 10 to 20 times. Then try passing a ball between your legs as you make a scissor-like motion with both legs. Move quicker and try doing it with your eyes shut.

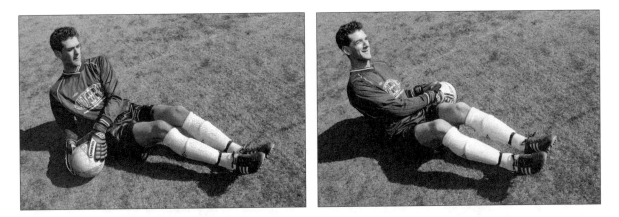

➤ Sit down with your legs together but knees bent with your back at a 45-degree angle to the ground. Raise your feet 4 inches (10 cm.) from the ground while keeping your legs as straight as possible and touch the ball from one side of your body to the other.

➤ You can try the same exercise (shown below), but with your heels three to four inches off the ground. Try lifting both legs over the top of the ball without touching the ground with your heels.

➤ Next, lie flat on your back with a ball between your legs. Lock your hands around the ankles of a partner who is standing directly over top of you and behind your shoulders. Raise the ball off the ground to touch your partner's hands and lower the ball locked in your legs down to six inches from the ground. Return to touch the partner's hands with your toes. Avoid bending your legs at all times. Repeat up to 15 times.

➤ When you're ready, put a ball between your legs in the v-sit position and play throw and catch with your partner, but only use your feet. It's awkward to start, but once you get the hang of it, you may not want to stop! Next, try to add a second ball in the hands, so the routine goes from feet to feet, and hands to hands.

1.4   Getting a Grip: Ball Handling

Goalkeepers can prepare for the important demands of playing the position with these exercises.

Exercise 1: SEATED HANDLING EXERCISE (All Levels)
➤ Start seated, holding a ball and facing your partner, who is on their knees with a ball in their hands. At the same time, one rolls the ball on the ground while the other tosses it in the air. Keep your eyes on the ball you're catching.

Exercise 2: BALL EXCHANGE (All Levels)
➤ Work as a pair with another goalkeeper and one ball. Stand back-to-back separated by a half-step. Perform a figure eight, a trunk rotation and an over and under. Place your feet shoulder-width apart and face forward. Rotate your trunk while your feet are still.

TIP: ❯ If you're an advanced goalkeeper, you can also try using a medicine ball.

Exercise 3: HANDLING DIAMOND (All Levels)

➤ Form a diamond with your partner and another pair of goalkeepers. Face each other, but be two or three steps apart. All of you should sit with your legs straight out in front of the body and place a ball in the hands of one of the goalkeepers. Hold your hands up to receive the ball and play catch. Make eye contact with each goalkeeper or call his or her name before you throw the ball. When you're ready, add a second ball.

Exercise 4: GOALKEEPER SIT-UPS (All Levels)

➤ Face another goalkeeper and be a step apart. Both of you start doing sit-ups. Between each sit-up, exchange the ball by tossing it into each other's hands and touch it to the ground over your head with two hands on the ball. Try adding another pair of goalkeepers to form a diamond. Keep your balls from colliding as they cross the centre of the diamond.

Exercise 5: DIAMOND SIT-UPS (Intermediate and Advanced)

➤ This is where it gets difficult. Each goalkeeper should have a ball and remain in the diamond formation. Continue sit-ups and pass the ball with your partner. One player must throw the ball along the ground, while the other player will toss it in the air. Be careful not to collide balls with the other pair in your diamond.

Exercise 6: CUSHIONING THE BALL (Intermediate and Advanced)

➤ Get ready in a push-up position to receive the ball with either your left or right hand; cushion it without letting it hit your body. Return it to the server. When you're ready, make a figure eight with the ball around your stationary arm before you return it to the server.

Exercise 7: ARM WRESTLING
(Intermediate and Advanced)

➤ Face your partner in the same push-up position mentioned above; the object is to use your arms to pull your partner to the ground. Make sure that neither of you places your knees on the ground while performing this exercise.

Exercise 8: STANDING BALL EXCHANGE (Intermediate and Advanced)

➤ Stand facing another goalkeeper and be several steps apart. Hold a ball with the opposite hand from your partner. Toss the balls back and forth at the same time as your partner. Do not drop the balls or allow them to hit your body. Begin with underhand throws from the waist and progress to a baseball-style throw in the air. Don't throw too hard — you're not a pitcher throwing strikes.

➤ When you're ready, try to move across the field in tandem while doing this exercise.

Exercise 9: BALL ROTATION (Intermediate and Advanced)

➤ Stand and make a small triangle with two other goalkeepers or a square with three others. Everyone in the formation should have a ball. Play catch within the group by throwing the ball in the same direction as the rest of the group. Rotate clockwise or counter-clockwise. Players stand about three or four metres apart and throw their ball in the same direction around the square.

➤ When you're ready, try moving your bodies in the same direction as you are tossing the balls. Focus only on the ball you are receiving and look through the corners of your eyes to sense where the partner you are throwing the ball towards is located.

Players stand about 3 – 4 metres apart and throw ball in the same direction around the square.

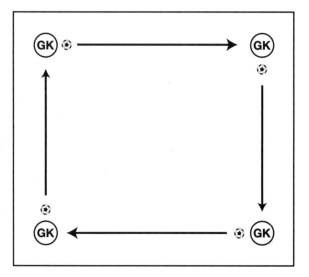

1.5 Goalkeeper Warm-Up

Goalkeepers need to feel the ground and the ball. Like anything in life, you'll have to build your skills from the ground up.

BEGINNERS

You'll need to learn how to fall to the ground on top of and behind the ball. You can't avoid getting dirty. What you want to avoid is letting the ball go by.

➤ Pull the ball into your chest and fall to the ground on the outside of your shoulder.

➤ Tuck your top leg over the ball, while lying on the ground with the ball in your chest.

➤ Get a ball and sit facing your goalkeeper trainer or coach.

➤ Try starting in a kneeling position and land on the outside of your knee with an elbow tucked in tight to the body and onto the outside of the shoulder.

➤ Avoid taking one arm away to put it down on the ground before landing because you must secure the ball into the chest and become comfortable contacting the ground in this manner. Otherwise, you risk losing control of the ball. (shown below)

➤ Next, while standing, take two steps behind and two steps to the side of the ball and try

collapsing on the stationary ball. You should land on the outside of the knee, the outside of the hip and the soft part of your shoulder. Tuck your elbow into your body and land on the outside of your shoulder and attack the ball in a forward manner. Repeat 15 to 20 times.

INTERMEDIATE AND ADVANCED

➤ Sit on the ground directly in front of the *server* (one or two metres away) who will toss balls to you from side to side. Eventually, move to your knees, then squat and finally stand.

SITTING

➤ When you're in the seated position, catch the ball with your thumbs behind the centre of the ball and place your hands on either side. Keep your back to the goal and collapse on the outside of your shoulder. Bring the ball into your chest and tuck the top knee over the ball to bring your body forward, thus protecting the ball from an attacker.

KNEELING

➤ Start with your hands up and palms facing the server. Don't rest on your heels. Collapse onto the outside of your hip, then to the outside of your shoulder, while holding the ball tightly in your chest. Fall as far *forward* as possible to receive the ball at the *earliest* point.

➤ Finish with the ball in your chest and tuck your top knee over the ball. Move your body forward because you don't want to curl around the ball. That would make it harder to get back on your feet quickly.

SQUATTING

➤ Start with your knees bent, hands facing out towards the server and your body at a three-quarter stance, so you're not collapsing from a full upright position. Receive each ball with your thumbs behind the centre of the ball and hands on either side. Collapse on the outside of the knee with the ball stowed in the chest, then to the outside of the hip and shoulder. Fall as far forward as possible to receive the ball and finish with it in your chest. Tuck the top knee over the ball to protect from an attacker.

➤ Get back on your feet without using your hands to push off the ground. Think of yourself as a spring rebounding into action.

STANDING

➤ Start in the goalkeeper's ready position and face the server who will serve balls in the air to your sides. Collapse on the outside of your knee, then the hip and onto the outside of your shoulder. Always attack the ball in a *forward* motion.

➤ When the ball is played along the ground, change the position of your hands. Put your bottom hand directly behind the ball, bring the top hand down on top of the ball and use the ground as your "third hand" to stop the ball.

The Goalkeeper's Ready Position

As a goalkeeper, you always need to be ready for the attacking team to press forward at you. There are five keys to the goalkeeper's ready position:

1) Hands up at the waist with your palms facing out towards the shooter;
2) Bend your knees;
3) Feet apart the same width as your shoulders;
4) Stand on the balls of your feet;
5) Be hunched, slightly forward, with your eyes focused on the ball.

*The position of your hands will vary,
just as the space differs between you and the ball-carrying attacker.*

Exercise 1: SEATED BALL HANDLING (All Levels)

➤ Begin seated directly in front of the server, placing your hands on top of your knees in a comfortable position. The ball is thrown at your face for you to catch and return to the server. Each time, place your palms flat on your knees. This helps you stay concentrated. Repeat 60 times.

Exercise 2: TWO-BALL JUGGLING (Advanced)

➤ The server must hold a ball at the waist while standing directly in front of another goalkeeper who is seated holding a ball. When the server tosses a ball to the side for you, toss your ball back to the server. Continue to rotate from side to side while exchanging balls. Make sure the goalkeeper sits up and back down to the side each time to stretch their abdominal muscles. When you collect the ball in your hands, bring it to your chest.

Exercise 3: CROSSOVERS (Advanced)

➤ Sit two steps apart from another goalkeeper. Hold the ball and lie on your side. As you sit up, toss the ball to your partner who will receive the ball and collapse on a shoulder. After your partner gains control and finishes with the ball in their chest, they will sit up and toss the ball for you to take a turn. Repeat 30 times or for a set amount of time and eventually add a second ball to the exercise.

Exercise 4: CATCH AND COLLAPSE (All levels)

➤ Face another goalkeeper two steps apart. Toss the ball back and forth, collapsing on the outside of your knee, hip, elbow and shoulder. Before receiving the ball, make sure to return to a standing position.

1.6 Receiving Balls

➤ Be in a ready position with your feet shoulder-width apart. One method is for you to go down on one knee to receive a ball rolling along the ground. Place your upper body and shoulders square to the ball. Turn either knee to the side and keep the other knee as far back as possible from the ball. Bend your body forward to pick up the ball.

➤ You can also stay standing with your legs straight and bent at the waist to pick-up the ball. Either way works as long as your body is behind the path of the ball.

➤ Your hands must be positioned so your fingertips point down at the ground, thumbs out at the sides and palms facing the direction of the ball. Together, your hands should form the shape of a shovel, ready to dig the ball.

➤ Finally, always secure the ball in your chest to complete the save.

RECEIVING BALLS IN THE CHEST

➤ When a ball is struck above your knees and below your neck, place as much of your body behind the ball as possible. Stand balanced in the ready position. Reach out with your forearms parallel to your body with your arms at the sides of the ribs. It's always best to use your body to cushion the impact of the ball. Any part of your body behind the ball helps keep the ball from entering the goal.

FRONT SCOOP

➤ The front scoop is a save where you will place your body behind the ball and fall forward with the ball tucked into your chest. Collect the ball and land with your knees touching the ground first, followed by the chest and finishing with your body flat on the ground.

➤ This type of save can be useful when you need to collect a ball that's bouncing towards your midsection, between the knees and waist. By getting behind the ball and falling forward, the ball won't end up in the goal if it does take an unusual bounce.

RECEIVING BALLS AT THE FACE

➤ When collecting a ball shot at your face, the position of your hands differs from that of lower shots. Your palms must face forward as your hands make the shape of the letter-W. Spread your fingers to cover the sides of the ball and keep your thumbs behind the centre of the ball with a small gap between them. Reach out with your arms to receive the ball at the *earliest* point. Make sure to *cushion* the ball as you receive it with your elbows bent. Use your fingertips and palms to cushion the ball as it arrives. Finally, hold it in your hands and hug it in your chest.

RECEIVING HIGH BALLS

➤ Always try to catch the ball *at* the *highest point* possible, with your arms fully extended. Place your hands behind the ball, forming the letter-W; you must be able to watch the ball enter your hands. Shout "keeper!" in a loud and clear voice to tell your defenders and the attackers that you are going for the ball.

➤ The correct way to leap or jump is the one leg take-off which provides upward movement for greater height.

➤ Begin your leap or jump off the proper foot, with the outside leg towards the field thrust upward and bent at the knee. Keep your leg closest to the goal straight.

This is exactly the same as performing a lay-up in basketball.

➤ If a collision happens when you challenge for the ball, keep your leg bent in a raised position to guard the goal from aggressive attackers.

Note left: This is the *wrong* position to catch the ball – always catch the ball at the highest possible point and make sure that you are able to see the ball.

Karina LeBlanc

Karina LeBlanc started playing soccer when she was 12 and alternated between goal and the forward line for two years. Her coach liked the way she scored goals at one end of the field and saved them at the other. Karina, who is from British Columbia, plays for Canada's National Women's team and the Boston Breakers of the WUSA league in the United States, the top professional women's league in the world.

My most memorable save:
In sudden death overtime where I made a reaction save to a ball that came from about four metres out.

My most embarrassing moment:
Once, from a pass back, I had a ball take a bad bounce on me right as I was about to kick it, and it rolled right into the net!

The benefits of practising footwork:
Fast footwork allows you to react better to situations that occur in front of you. Fast footwork allows you to change directions quicker, and to move faster around and off your line. It also allows you to be more agile with the ball at your feet. It is one of the most important aspects of goalkeeping.

My favourite footwork activities:
We use speed ladders that are made of cloth and we do about 30 different drills where you alternate from side-to-side, front to back, one leg or two. There are so many drills; if you are creative you can come up with your own. The whole point is to have your feet moving quickly. We also do a lot of moving from side-to-side in the goal with the addition of the ball so that you are staying focused on the ball at all times, yet enhancing your footwork skills.

My words of advice to young goalkeepers:
To be a great goalkeeper you have to be mentally tough. You have to be able to handle every moment that goes on in games, both the good and the bad. Unfortunately, if we make a mistake that results in a goal everyone notices it — unlike the other field players. You have to find a way to deal with those moments, maybe by forgetting about it until the game is over and then, if necessary, analyze it. To be the best, you may then have to do additional work to correct bad habits. Maybe, pull your coach aside and ask him to help you with your weaknesses; then you'll be confident knowing that the same mistake will not happen again.

Karina LeBlanc in Gold Cup action October, 2002.
— Photo © Dale MacMillan

Iker Casillas, Spanish goalkeeper, in action at the 2002 World Cup.

— PHOTO © DALE MACMILLAN

Footwork, Flying and Focus

Sports do not build character. They reveal it.

— John Wooden

The most memorable save of my career happened during a 1990 game in the Canadian Soccer League. I was playing for the Victoria Vistas against the Vancouver Eighty-Sixers.

Vancouver veteran Dale Mitchell lined up to take a free kick from the left side of the penalty area, 20 metres from the goal. Mitchell was renowned for his ability to bend the ball around a wall. Four of my teammates set a wall to protect the near post. I positioned myself on the opposite side of the goal. The first Vancouver player ran over the top of the ball to distract our team. When Dale struck the ball, it bent around the outside of the wall to the near post. I had to move across the face of the goal without seeing where the ball was (the wall blocked my vision), and I desperately dove to block as much of the goal as possible. Suddenly, I felt the ball deflect off my body and saw it hit the goalpost and back into the goalkeeper's area.

"Brødsgaard, Brødsgaard, what a save!" screamed the TV announcer. The ensuing scramble for the rebound ended when an attacker shot the ball and it deflected over the crossbar. Then it was my turn to relax and take a goal kick.

2.1 Footwork and Balance

Goalkeepers are the only players on the field who can play the ball with their hands. But goalkeepers should never overlook the importance of footwork.

As a goalkeeper you move by shuffling along the field, touching the ground only with the studs or soles of your boots. Be on the balls of your feet with your body hunched slightly forward. The posture of the body should be erect. Do not cross your legs while working in the goal. You may have to change direction quickly and could easily trip or stumble if your legs were crossed. Always keep your hands up and palms facing out towards the shooter when moving across the goal.

Exercise 1: SIDEWAYS FOOT MOVEMENT (All Levels)

➤ Moving backwards and forwards will only take you so far. You need to go side-to-side to follow the play. Place up to six markers, one metre apart. Side step through the line of markers in the ready position. Place a ball beyond the last marker to collapse on and save, falling forwards to attack the ball. Work both directions.

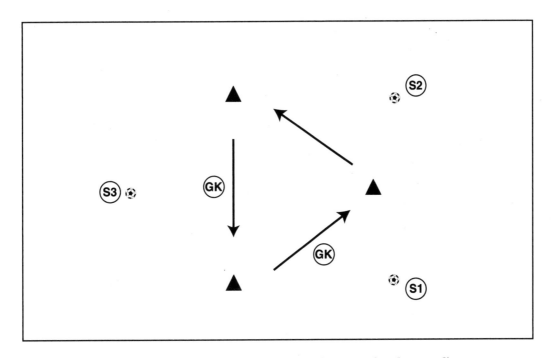

Exercise 2: FOOTWORK TRIANGLE (Intermediate and Advanced)

➤ Use three markers, five metres apart, to form a large triangle with three mini-goals. Then place three servers directly in front of each goal, approximately five metres out. The goalkeeper moves across the face of the goal and receives a ball in the chest. Move around the triangle clockwise or counter-clockwise four more times. Listen for an instruction from the server before moving to the correct position to receive the ball.

➤ Number each of the servers (1, 2, 3). The goalkeeeper must listen for an instruction before moving to the correct position to receive the ball. Always face the server without turning your back to the ball. Make sure the server allows time for you to arrive in front of the goal line before serving the ball into the chest.

➤ As an extra drill, place a ball in front of either the near or far post on each mini-goal and attack the ball while moving across the face of the goal.

POINTS TO REMEMBER

1) Turn to face the server without turning your back on the ball. Always be in full view of the server's ball;

2) Make sure the server allows time for you to arrive in front of the goal line before serving the ball into the chest.

Exercise 3: DUMMY BALL EXERCISES (Intermediate and Advanced)

➤ In the first exercise, start on the near post and side-step across to touch a ball placed in the mid-goal area; then, step back to the near post to catch and collapse on the ball served in the air or along the ground.

➤ Next, get in the same position, but tip or deflect the ball away from the goal. Learn to deflect the ball with control, using both hands. You can also ask an additional person to go to the side of the goal as a target to receive the deflected ball and return it to the server to keep the drill moving.

➤ Finally, try starting on the near post and side-step across to the ball in the mid-goal area and "catch and collapse" on the ball served in the air or on the ground. React very quickly to the opposite side of the goal for a second save.

1) Focus on the server, not the ball, and look through the corners of your eyes to sense where the dummy ball is located;

2) Make the first step off the ball in a forward direction;

3) Drive off the inside leg for power. Kick the top leg forward while in the air to provide momentum.

Exercise 4:
JERRY'S TWO-STEP
(Intermediate and Advanced)

➤ The goalkeeper and server each hold a ball, facing each other at a distance of two metres. Step side-to-side while exchanging balls with each other at waist height. Concentrate on good ball-handling skills, proper balance and coordination. The goalkeeper coach can count the number of touches on the ball and push you to work harder as you become comfortable with the exercise.

➤ Next, try standing and switch diving from one side to the other, continually with two balls. Hold on to your ball until you have returned to your feet and are prepared to make another save. Finally, perform the same exercise by deflecting the ball at targets on each side.

1) Do not cross your legs or allow the distance between your feet to be greater than shoulder width;

2) Always move each foot on its own to avoid hopping and to maintain control of body movement.

Exercise 5: FOOTWORK PRETZEL (Intermediate and Advanced)

➤ This drill will help you become familiar with how you move in the goal. Place four markers a metre away from each other to create a box. Begin at the rear of the square, facing your goalkeeper coach directly in front of the box, standing five-to-six metres away.

➤ In the first exercise, step through the centre of the box to receive a ball in your chest in front of the first two markers (exercise a). After the save, move to the right around the outside of the box always facing the server. Return back through the centre to receive the next ball. Alternate going to the left or right around the outside of the box (exercise b).

➤ Place another ball in your hands, as well as the server's. Move through the box holding your ball to exchange with the server each time in the middle of the box. Begin at the rear of the area, step into the middle of the box and dive at an angle (between markers) to make a save by diving to the side. Repeat the same pattern of movement by returning to your feet and repeating the same on the other side. When you're ready, add a second ball and start diving.

➤ This exercise can also introduce the high ball. Ask to be served the ball in front of you at a height that challenges you to take the ball at the highest point with your arms fully extended, jumping off the ground with one leg and protecting yourself each time with the correct knee in the air.

➤ Change the distance between the front and rear markers for greater depth in your area to cover. The emphasis is on back-peddling with power and control (exercise c).

POINTS TO REMEMBER

1) Save each ball as you're going forward and dive at an angle to receive the ball at the earliest point;

2) Always grab the ball in your hands and hug it into your chest before touching the ground.

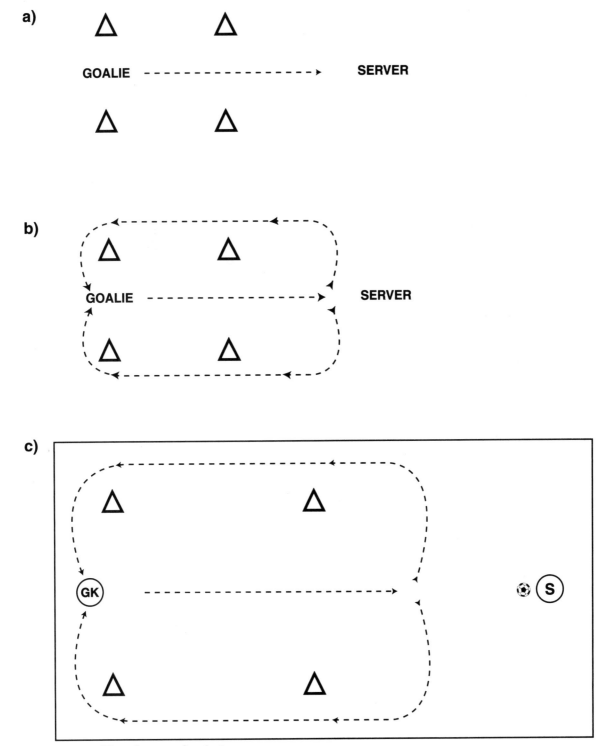

10 metre spacing between cones

Exercise 6: FOOTWORK RELAYS (Intermediate and Advanced)

Form a group with three or four other goalkeepers in a small line before the six hurdles (20 cm. high) or make the stations with a row of floppy markers or cones. Space each hurdle or marker one metre apart. Progress through the following exercises. Once you're familiar with the progression create a competition by challenging another group of goalkeepers to a race.

a)

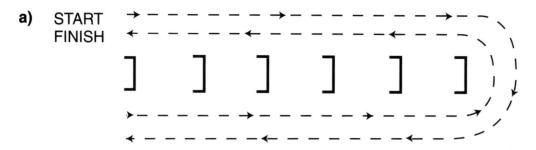

1) Facing sideways, move around the outside of the area by shuffling your feet;

b)

2) Facing sideways, but running forwards and backwards through the center of the space created by the two hurdles, or markers;

c)

3) Facing sideways, run over the top of the hurdles by placing the lead foot down, followed by the second foot in each space provided by the hurdle or set of markers. When you reach the end of the set, try to make contact with one foot before proceeding back through the remainder of the course.

POINTS TO REMEMBER

1) Stay on the balls of your feet;
2) The arms should be used for balance;
3) Bring your knees up as high as possible in exercise three.

Exercise 7: SPEED LADDER (Intermediate and Advanced)

The speed ladder is an excellent way to increase your foot-speed and balance. Beginners will start by looking down at their feet when doing these exercises. Intermediates must look up, away from the ladder. Advanced goalkeepers look at the coach for a reaction cue.

The speed ladder is a contraption which has 12 steps; each step is 16 inches x 16 inches (30 cm. x 30 cm.) laying flat on the ground. The idea is to place one foot or both feet in between each "rung."

GOALKEEPER →	R		L		R		L

1) Run facing forward touching every second square, then every square and finally every third square;

2) Hop on the right foot, touching each square. Do the same, but use your left foot. Touch every second square;

3) Facing forwards, hop with both feet together, touching each second square. First try for height, then for speed. Then try touching every square and finally every third square;

L/R	L/R	L/R	L/R	L/R	L/R	L/R

↑

GOALKEEPER

4) Facing sideways, move through the ladder placing each foot one at a time in each square, right foot first. Work both directions;

GOALKEEPER →

5) Hop forwards with both feet, alternating touching the right foot and left foot in the centre. Do the same, but go backwards.

6) Step into the square with the right foot, then the left foot and back out with the right foot. Then, lead into the next square with the left foot and progress down the ladder in this pattern.

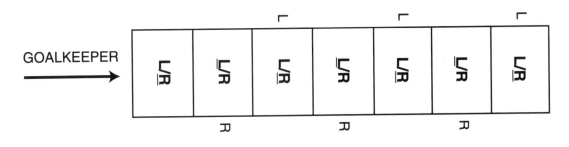

7) As the goalkeeper progresses through the exercises given, place one or two balls down the side of the ladder with a two metre gap from the area the goalkeeper is working in. The instructor will give a verbal command, such as "go" while the goalkeeper is moving through the ladder with a specified pattern. At this time, the goalkeeper can either explode forwards to scoop the ball into the chest or stretch to make a diving save.

ball into the chest or stretch to make a diving save.

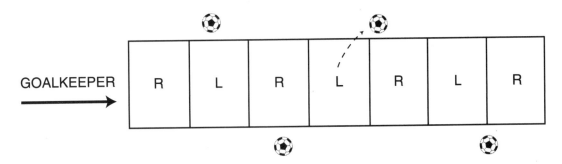

2.2 Collapsing and Diving Techniques

As a goalkeeper, you'll be ready to train at a higher level after completing your age-related warm-up. The easiest way to be comfortable and confident in performing these exercises is to begin without a ball. Remember, landing on the ground can be an intimidating experience. If you find it difficult to start from a standing position, then start on your knees, or even from a seated position.

TIP: A sand-pit can be a great place to practise landing and diving, as well as a wrestling or gymnastics mat, because they're softer than soccer fields.

Exercise 1: STATIONARY BALL DRILL (Beginner and Intermediate)

➤ To understand the proper way to collapse, stand in a small goal. Either use two balls or two markers for posts, no greater than five steps on either side of you to the nearest post. Stand in the centre of the goal in the ready position, ready to collapse on command. Another player or coach stands five metres in front of the goal to tell you to collapse toward one of the posts. Return to the centre of the goal each time for a new instruction.

➤ As you become more comfortable at collapsing, try jumping straight up and down in the middle of the goal before the command. Next, start by lying flat on your stomach and return to your feet after collapsing on command. When you're ready, turn the opposite way. Then, on command, turn and face your coach in the ready position and collapse as directed.

➤ Once you're able to collapse to the ground without a ball, then you're ready to incorporate a ball into the above exercise.

POINTS TO REMEMBER

1) Don't turn over on your weak side and land without your body behind the ball.
2) Always face the server or shooter;
3) Return to the middle of the goal quickly and under control and wait for further instructions in the ready position.

Exercise 2: SECOND SAVE POSITION (Intermediate and Advanced)

➤ Lie on the ground in the collapse position. Make sure your upper body is slightly forward of your hips so that they will be able to explode out towards the ball. While lying in the collapse position, the server drops the ball slightly out to the side and in front of you. The object is to push your body off the ground and smother the ball, as if you had made one save and had to make a second save to block or smother the ball. Always alternate sides.

➤ This drill can be done with one or two other goalkeepers and a second ball, starting from the same point. Bounce the balls in, and vary the number of times the ball is allowed to bounce.

Exercise 3: CONSECUTIVE EXPLOSIVE DIVING (All Levels)

➤ From a squatting position, work across the penalty area, make a diving save and each time toss the ball to the server as you return to your feet. Be ready to make another save to the same side. Continue until you reach the end of the penalty area. Rest for a moment, then perform the same drill in the opposite direction.

➤ Try the same drill, but with two balls.

Exercise 4: DIVING OVER THE DUMMY (Intermediate and Advanced)

➤ Have one player lying face down on the ground, next to you and facing where the shot will be taken. Dive across the dummy and touch the coach's hand. Switch sides after six times. If you can dive across the dummy and collapse onto the ground, add a ball and try it again.

➤ In the Advanced version of this drill, step away from the dummy and touch a marker before diving back across the dummy to make the save.

POINTS TO REMEMBER

1) Face your feet forwards or at the server, not to the side you'll be diving towards;

2) Don't put your hands on the ground to cushion your landing;

3) Don't let your feet be the first part of you to touch the ground after diving over the dummy;

4) Hug the ball in your chest. Always secure the ball in this manner before contacting the ground, to prevent the ball from being jarred loose.

Exercise Five: NUMBER DIAMOND (Advanced)

➤ Place four markers in the shape of a diamond, five meters apart. Start in the center of the area and respond to the instructions given by your coach. Each cone will be given a number and you must react by touching the cone and returning to the middle of the area as quickly as possible. The ball is served at you each time you return to the center of the diamond. Always look at the ball, not the server.

➤ Next, save the ball at each cone. Which means you'll be diving from side-to-side, with high balls going forwards and backwards. The service to the side begins along the ground, but then gets harder when the ball is tossed in the air at waist-height or volleyed at you.

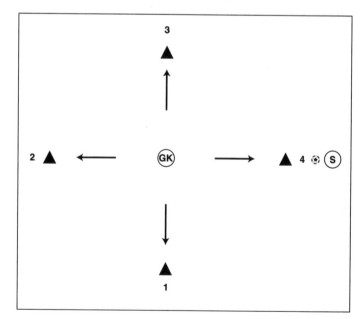

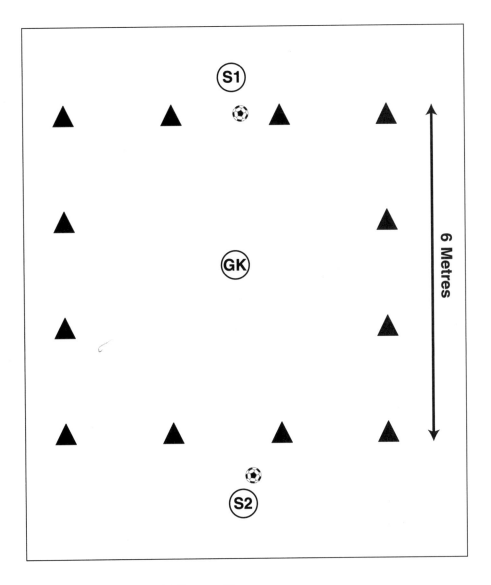

Exercise Six: PENALTY BOX (Advanced)

➤ Set up a square, six metres by six metres. You'll work for 40 seconds and rest for 20 seconds, completing two exercises in a row. The server tosses the ball into the box with a variety of services. You're challenged to prevent the ball from landing on the ground.

➤ Next, add a server on each side of the box and work around the area. Try receiving two balls from each server before moving to the opposite side of the box.

➤ Service can also be along the ground where the goalkeeper must save the ball before it leaves the box.

2.3 Reaction Drills (for Advanced Goalkeepers)

These drills are all for Advanced Goalkeepers to test their reaction by adding a second save for the goalkeeper to react to after the initial ball has been served.

Exercise 1: RAPID FIRE

➤ Line-up a row of balls across the face of the goal, at a distance of 10 metres. The server will play one ball at a time, working down the row, striking from one side of the goal to the other. You must get a chance to return to your feet and react to the next ball before the next ball is served to the opposite side of the goal.

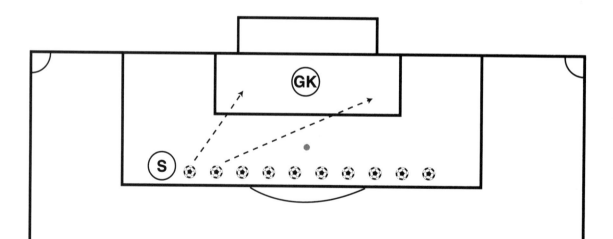

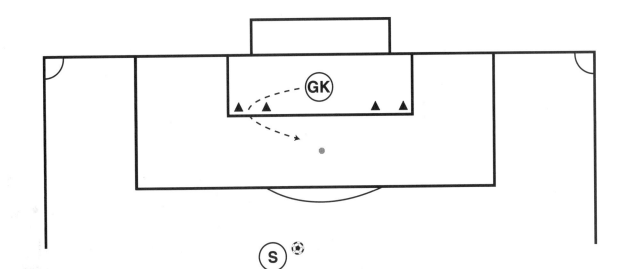

Exercise 2: GATES DRILL

➤ This drill helps you to keep proper balance when moving from side to side in the goal. Place a ball or markers on an angle at a two-metre interval at each side of the goalkeeper's box for you to step through before making each save.

➤ Begin the drill in the centre of the goal, on the line. Wait for directions from the server, who points to the gate you must pass through. Move through the gates before returning to the center of the goal to react and save the ball played in by the server from the penalty area.

➤ Always shuffle your feet across the face of the goal and don't cross your legs.

Exercise 3: TIP AND SAVE

➤ This drill is an excellent way to regain your balance and find the ball as quickly as possible before reacting to make the save.

Place a server on each side of the goal. Begin by facing the goal and jump up to tip the ball served to you over the crossbar. As soon as you make the first save, turn and face the second server at the top of the penalty area who will strike the ball at goal.

Exercise 4: TEN REACTION SAVES

➤ This drill, done in sequences of ten, is an excellent way to test your reactions and speed in collecting the ball from the server. React when the server, who is standing six metres in front of you, plays in the ball. Once each save is made, return to your feet to react to the next ball from the server. Focus on footwork and speed of recovery from the ground to your feet. Ask the server to send it to you from side to side, in the air or along the ground, or directly in front of you. That way you'll have to collapse forward on the ball. Ask for high balls to each side and even add defensive pressure as you take the ball.

PAUL STURROCK IS A SCOTTISH SOCCER LEGEND. The Aberdeen native played his entire 15-year professional career with Dundee United where he scored 109 goals in 385 games. He also played for his country 20 times.

Since the end of his playing career, he has managed St. Johnstone, Dundee United and Plymouth Argyle. I met him at a soccer camp in Shawnigan Lake, British Columbia and I'm proud to say he's a friend. He offered me this exercise to share with you.

IT'S CALLED STURROCK'S SPECIAL.

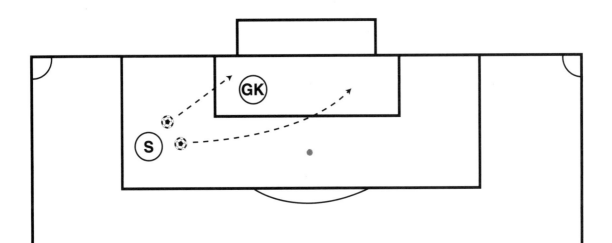

Exercise 5: STURROCK'S SPECIAL

➤ This drill works on cutting down your angle of approach for the second ball, which means taking it at the earliest point, and not fading away into the goal to receive the ball. Place two balls on the ground at an angle, eight metres from the goal. Have the first ball played along the ground to the near post for you to save. Complete this save before reacting to the next ball.

➤ The second ball is served in the air to the back post. Stay as big as possible to block the goal and increase your success rate for keeping the ball out of the old onion sack! Try attacking the first ball on the ground, while the second ball will be played to the other post at your body and in the air. Attack the ball and react to the service by diving across the face of the goal.

➤ When you make the save with
the correct forward motion, the
ball will always go away from
the goal. Move across the face
of the goal with your palms
facing out to the shooter,
because you never know when
you may be called to make a
reaction save!

*Note: this shows the incorrect
way, as he's not taking the ball
at the earliest point.*

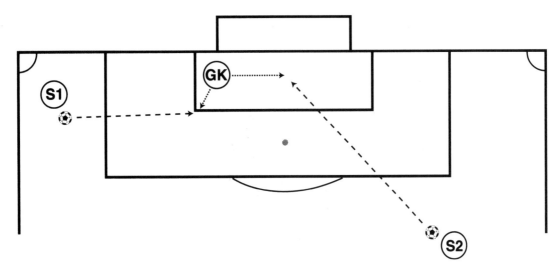

Exercise 6: NICCI'S CROSSOVER DRILL

➤ This drill will help force you to attack the ball by making the save at the earliest point and communicating while moving across the face of the goal. Stand beside the first post and face the server who will play a ball along the ground to the edge of the six-yard box. As you save the ball, a second ball is played in the air to the second post after you have returned to your feet.

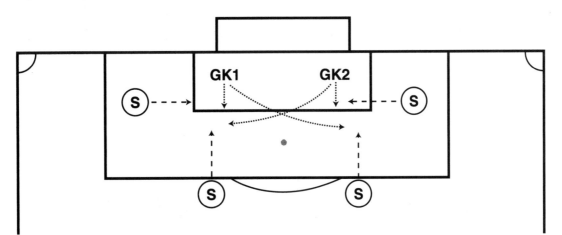

➤ Next, try standing beside one of the posts and invite another goalkeeper to stand on the other side of the goal. Once the first save is completed, cross in front of the goal to react to the second ball played to the far post by the server. Attack the ball, be aggressive and communicate with the other goalkeeper. Decide who is going to cross in front and who is going to cross in behind to make the save.

Erin McLeod

Erin McLeod began to play soccer when she was five, and found goalkeeping was her favourite position by age 12. She loved the satisfaction of making a save and hearing people cheer. The Alberta native was Canada's starting goalkeeper for the 2002 FIFA U19 Women's World Championship. Erin helped her team to a second place finish. She is fulfilling her soccer dreams as a member of Canada's U19 team and National Women's team.

My most memorable moment:
When I played with the World Cup team in France against Australia. It was my first game with the World Cup squad. I had a terrible warm-up and was a bit worried. Once I was out there, I felt like I was on top of the world, everything seemed so clear and made sense. I got a shutout.

My favourite part of playing goal:
The feeling after making a save. My heart starts racing and I get this big smile on my face. I just feel completely content, that's why I continue to play the game – because for the split second that I'm making the save all that exists is the ball and I.

My most embarrassing moment:
Was in a game against Portugal with a junior and World Cup mixed team. I made a communication and decision error, which led to being scored on by one of my defenders' pass backs. Not only was it embarrassing, I felt like I had let my team down because I went from having complete control to losing it in one second. This is one of the reasons why I've learned to always be on my toes!

The first thing that goes across my mind after a save:
I get this true feeling of confidence, like I'm on top of the world. After I make a save I look for the transition. I try and get up and look up the field. After this job is done I take a second to appreciate what I've just done (I review it in my head so I can do it again). Then I focus back on the game.

How I prepare for breakaway saves before a game:
I visualize the striker taking a touch a bit too long or not under complete control. Once I recognize this I go in for the kill and see myself winning the ball.

What I do in training to prepare for the game situation:
I try to take what I'm learning and apply it to a game situation. Like taking a cross. I'll see myself taking the cross, visualize a team in front of me and see myself delivering the ball to someone on my team. In training I try to get enough possible situations I could possibly get, therefore in a game the situation is familiar and I'll know what to do.

Erin McLeod celebrates a penalty shootout victory at the 2002 FIFA
U19 Women's World Championship in Edmonton. — PHOTO © MICHAEL STAHLSCHMIDT

My best words of advice for young players:
I started playing soccer because my parents thought it would be a good experience for me. My love for the sport has kept me going and always wanting to be the best I can be stems from this love. My parents taught me that sport is supposed to be fun, and this is my advice too. Play or do something, put your whole heart and effort into it, but if it isn't fun you're wasting your time. Play soccer because you enjoy it and love it. Don't ever do something you don't want to do. Have dreams and set goals high. Believe in yourself, know when to go hard and when to take it easy. Nevertheless, most of all, enjoy yourself, enjoy life, and have fun!

Erin McLeod in action at the 2002 FIFA U19 Women's World Championship.
— PHOTO © MICHAEL STAHLSCHMIDT

3

Making the Save and Starting the Attack

Regardless of how you feel inside, always try to look like a winner.
— Arthur Ashe

INTRODUCTION

There is one area of the game that challenges goalkeepers more than any other — kicking the ball, either from their hands or off the ground. All my life, I have taken pride in striking the ball. It's a habit of mine to stay late after practice and kick the ball back and forth with a teammate. Even today, as coaches, we enjoy the feeling of striking a good ball.

In my playing days my preference was to dropkick the ball, rather than punt it high downfield. I have always felt the dropkick is more direct, more accurate and places the other team under greater pressure.

One of my most valuable lessons came when I was 20. Gordon Hill, the former Nova Scotia Clippers Head Coach was a member of the 1976 English FA CUP-winning Manchester United. He provided these simple instructions for success:

— line-up your body behind the ball with the hips and shoulders square to your intended target;

— take two steps ahead and swing directly through the middle of the ball;

— avoid coming across the body with your kicking leg when contacting the ball;

— focus on control rather than power.

Many years later during my coaching career I was making a video version of *Guarding The Goal*. I must have hit 3,000 balls over the two-day production. By the time we were finished, I was able to control the ball while striking it toward goal plus dropkicking the ball like never before. It came because of all the repetitions in a short period of time. I guess you never stop learning about the game.

3.1 Breakaways

Preventing the attacker from scoring on a breakaway can be difficult for any goalkeeper. It can be intimidating to dive head first at the attacker's feet to prevent a goal. A person who thinks twice before committing to the ground will likely be injured. Raw courage is the ability to make a bold decision and bravely challenge for the ball while knowing that you could be proven wrong. Before trying to take the ball away from an attacker on a breakaway, you must know a few key points.

➤ First, make yourself as big as possible in the challenge for the ball. Second, position yourself as close to the ball as possible and stay on your feet as long as possible before committing to the ground.

➤ Finally, you must win the ball or force the player wide of the goal, allowing your defenders to get behind the ball.

TIP: Make sure to lower the position of your hands as you approach the player who has the ball. This helps make you appear larger.

➤ Train for a "one versus one" situation by building your confidence with the following techniques:

Exercise 1: JERRY'S STAR DIVING DRILL (All Levels)

➤ One player lies down with feet spread apart and the goalkeeper stands with one foot inside and one foot outside before pushing off to make the save. Attack the ball by diving forward from the inside leg at the server's feet. If you dive to the server's right, then your left leg is between the dummy's legs, and the right leg is on the outside of the dummy's right leg. The opposite is true for the left side.

Note: This shows the power coming from the outside leg, which is the incorrect technique.

➤ The server should start slightly to one side of where you will dive, to force you to dive outwards, and forwards, attacking the ball. The server should drop the ball, allowing you to dive forward and attack the ball and make yourself as big as possible. Move as soon as the server drops the ball. If it bounces, don't let it bounce a second time. Switch sides.

➤ Next, the server dropkicks the ball, allowing you to come and win the ball off the server's feet. The server should make it easy to start, but make the services more challenging later.

POINTS TO REMEMBER

Avoid arching yourself when you dive — you should look like ski-jumper when flying through the air. Concentrate on attacking the ball and don't allow it to go under your body — take the most direct route.

Exercise 2: STRIKER VERSUS GOALKEEPER (All Levels)

➤ Place the ball between two players. The first player will act as the attacker and stand three to four metres away from the ball. As the goalkeeper, stand at a distance from the ball, but remain close enough to close on it before the attacker comes.

➤ The drill begins with a movement, in any direction, by the attacking player. Dive at the player's feet to block the ball, with your hands and chest aimed at the ball. Play continues if the ball is deflected.

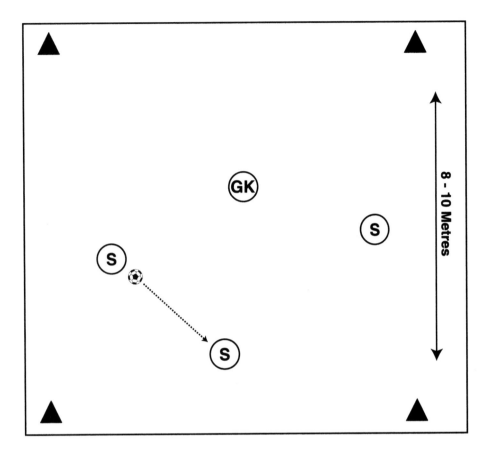

Exercise 3: THREE VERSUS ONE GOALKEEPER SCRIMMAGE (All Levels)

➤ Get inside a 10-metre by 10-metre square and play a three-on-one game of keep-away. The player in the middle will act as the goalkeeper who can get the ball by diving at the attacker's feet, just like on a breakaway. Count the number of interceptions you can make in 45 seconds while in the middle, and alternate goalkeepers. The goalkeepers on the outside must pass the ball and provide support for each other by moving into open space. The idea is to keep the ball away from the goalkeeper

Exercise 4: ONE VERSUS ONE SIMULATION
(Intermediate and Advanced)

➤ Place the markers two metres in front of the goal line and two metres from the side of each goalpost. Make two or three boxes, depending on the amount of players, stretching out from the front of the goalmouth, eight metres by 12 metres.

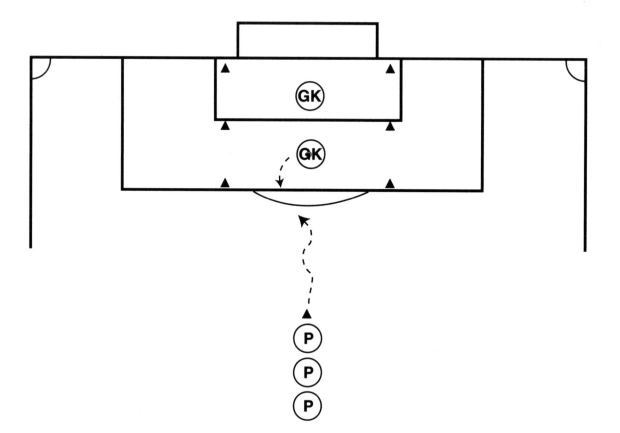

➤ A goalkeeper in each area will defend and prevent the attacker from going beyond their zone. When the player enters the first box, the goalkeeper must try to win the ball by diving at the player's feet. If the player keeps the ball and enters the second square, the first goalkeeper must allow the second goalkeeper to win the ball. Should an attacker defeat all the goalkeepers and score on the goal, each goalkeeper receives a penalty such as 10 push-ups.

➤ As soon as the attacker loses the ball to any goalkeeper, the next player in line should run at the first goalkeeper's square.

POINTS TO REMEMBER

1) If you're in the first square, work very hard for a short period of time. A maximum of 10 tries by the attackers is fine before switching spots;

2) Understand that the player dribbling the ball towards you will be as nervous approaching as you are in making the challenge.

3.2   Distribution

A smooth, flowing transition from defence to offence is essential in soccer. Skill and technique are crucial.

ROLLING

➤ Cup the ball in the palm of your hand, rested against the inside of your forearm. Step forward, point the non-throwing arm at your target and bend your waist forward. Bring your throwing arm down to release the ball on the ground, just like you're bowling. Don't let the ball bounce! Quick and accurate release is what you get when you do the underhand roll.

THROWING

➤ Throwing is the best way of distribution and has two advantages over kicking: accuracy and quick release. The chances for your team to keep the ball are greater when the goalkeeper can throw the ball with confidence.

BASEBALL THROW

➤ This is the best way to send the ball on wet ground and over medium distances (highly recommended for the Beginner goalkeeper). Hold the ball in your palm and let it go with a three-quarter side-arm motion similar to throwing a baseball. Snap your wrist forward, towards the target, to add speed to the throw. Point your non-throwing arm at the target and follow through after letting go of the ball.

OVERHAND THROW

➤ This is best throw for long distances. Cushion the ball against your forearm with a cupped wrist. Arch backward and snap your upper body forward at the waist. Step forward at the target and roll your shoulders over to let the ball go. Follow through with your entire body, not just the throwing arm (think of a basebal pitcher on the pitcher's mound). Throw the ball directly into the player's feet or lead them by bouncing the ball ahead, rolling it into their path. If the ball is spinning sideways in the air, correct your throwing technique and try to see a backspin on the ball.

KICKING

➤ The advantage of kicking is that it quickly sends the ball to your opponent's half of the field. You might gain possession when the ball is knocked down by the opposition and then begin the attack from this position on the field or send your player through on a breakaway with one direct pass. Strike the ball correctly and avoid using too much power!

GOAL KICK

➤ When you feel you're ready (usually by age 14) you should have the confidence to take your own goal kicks. There are three different options. The instep pass is good for a short ball, 15 to 20 metres. Or, chip the ball over the attackers to an open teammate. Driving the ball with your instep is the most common method to cover the greatest distance.

➤ As you approach the ball, place your non-kicking foot beside the ball, point the kicking foot toe down and strike through the centre of the ball with your shoelaces. Follow through with your arms out at the side of your body to stay balanced. Keep your eyes focused down on the ball until after the kick, as opposed to watching where you want it to go.

TIP: Develop a routine, so every time you kick the ball you are in control. Make a mental checklist, i.e. relax, eyes on the ball, kick through the centre of the ball, use control rather than power.

Note right: This is incorrect as the non-kicking foot is too far forward.

PUNTING OR DROPKICKING

➤ Start with the ball in your hands and point your hips in the direction you want to play the ball. Next, step forward and bring the ball down to your kicking foot by bending at the trunk and kick the ball from your hands. Strike through the centre of the ball to make it go higher and farther. Keep your eyes down on the ball until after the kick.

➤ For a dropkick, place the non-kicking foot to the side and contact the ball as it bounces off the ground using the top of your foot or shoelaces. The ball must be guided in a straight-forward kicking motion, to reduce the chance for error.

➤ You have six seconds to put the ball back in play. Take advantage of all the space in your penalty area — the element of surprise is in your favour. Before you receive the ball in your hands, take a snapshot of the field to help you decide what to do and run towards the front of the box. Leave enough room, up to five metres, from the edge of the penalty area and be sure you have the balance to punt or dropkick the ball. Always send the ball with the hope of keeping possession, not merely for distance or to clear it away from your opponent. Always try to play the ball into the player who is the best target on your team.

TIP: If your opponent isn't trying to mark you, take advantage of the space in front of you by rolling the ball along the ground outside of the penalty area. Then strike it as far as you can towards your opponent's end or to an intended target.

DEALING WITH PASS-BACKS

As a goalkeeper, you can also act like a sweeper, who calmly distributes the ball and begins the attack. When receiving the ball from a defender, make sure to gain control of the ball with a good first touch and open yourself up to see as much of the field as possible. Don't hold on to the ball unless it is completely safe to do so. The game of soccer does involve creativity, but not when you are the last person back in front of the goal! If you have to clear the ball, think safety first, not creativity. Clear for height and clear for distance.

Exercise 1: DEALING WITH PASS-BACKS (Intermediate and Advanced)

➤ Pair up with another goalkeeper, passing the ball back and forth from 10 metres with the inside of your feet. Take one touch to control the ball and set-up the pass before playing the ball back to your partner. Challenge yourself to receive the ball with one foot and play the ball with the other foot. Always control the ball in front of your body.

➤ Try increasing the gap to 20 metres. You may also chip the ball or drive it to your partner, who must control the ball without using hands. Always challenge yourself to strike the ball with different parts of your feet — learning to control the ball with a variety of strikes.

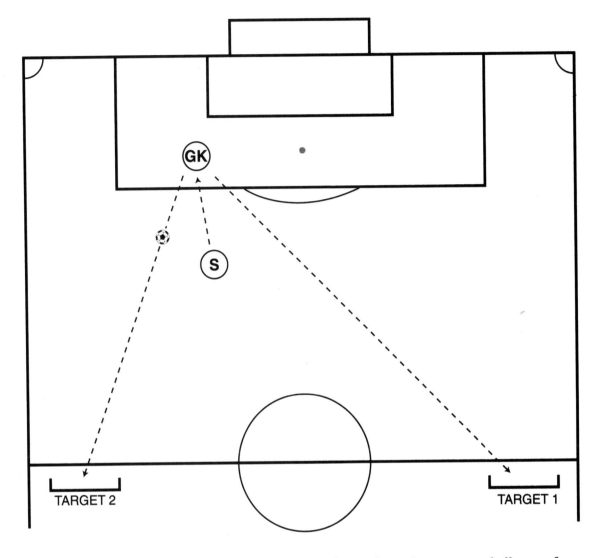

TARGET 2

TARGET 1

➤ Next, try one-touch passing with the inside of your feet. Then use two balls, one for each of you, to pass at the same time.

➤ When you're ready, receive a pass-back along the ground from the server and play the ball first time down the field into one of the identified targets. This way, you'll clear the ball high and away from danger.

➤ Finally, add a target player in the middle of the field, then on the sideline and finally on the opposite half. Ask an attacker to try marking you as you go to strike the ball. Ask your coach to vary the service so you can react to bouncing balls. Or control the ball with a part of your body before you try to clear it. Practise by switching from your right foot to your left foot, or the other way around.

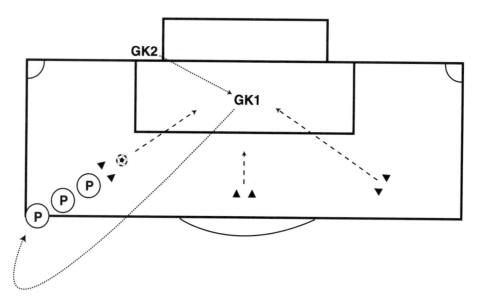

Exercise 2: BIG DADDY'S SPECIAL (Intermediate and Advanced)

➤ Identify three areas in front of the goal and ask the players to strike the ball one at a time towards the goalkeeper. After striking the ball, the players move as follows:
  • to the side of the goal (GK2)
  • then move from the side into the middle of the goal to make the save (GK1)
  • after making the save, the goalkeeper moves with the ball to the end of the shooting line (P).

➤ This becomes a competition when you make two teams. One group starts in the goal and each goalkeeper is rotated through every 30 to 45 seconds while the opponent strikes as many balls on goal for three minutes. Keep a running score between each of the teams to decide on a winner.

Exercise 3: FINDING THE SWEET SPOT (All Levels)

➤ Start directly in the goalkeeper's box, facing the goal. The server will play balls in from beside the post along the ground, in the air or bouncing for you to strike first time into the goal.

➤ Work from both sides of the goal, using both your right foot and left foot to contact the ball.

Exercise 4: GOAL KICK REPETITIONS (All Levels)

➤ Line up a row of balls in the goalkeeper's box, one metre apart. Work your way through the line of balls, and move as quickly as possible with control between each kick.

3.3   Collecting the Crossed Ball

Balance, timing and good judgment are keys to collecting a crossed ball.

Correct timing is necessary and the decision-making may be difficult. You must correctly judge the flight of the ball before committing to the cross. You can arrive for take-off too early or have to jump from a stationary position. If you leave the ground too early, the ball can end up travelling beyond you in the penalty area.

For correct timing, ask yourself: Is the ball still rising? When and where will it start to drop? Are there any attackers in the penalty area able to beat me to the ball? Once you decide to intercept the ball, take the most direct route and move forward quickly.

Always be aware of the attacking players. Be aware of the player crossing the ball, watch for the opposition entering the penalty area and take a position according to the amount of pressure on the ball, as well as the location of the player with the ball.

CROSSING DRILLS

Exercise 1: Static High Balls (All Levels)

➤ Begin standing between two others and have the ball served in the air from four metres away. The task is to collect the ball above your head with pressure from the others. You can also do this in the goalkeeper's box with an attacker to give you pressure. Have the server send the ball from the penalty spot, in the air as if it was volleyed. Grab the ball at its highest point and hug it to your body. Or, punch it away from danger.

Exercise 2:
PUNCHING FROM THE KNEES (Beginners)

➤ In order to build confidence, the goalkeeper begins on his/her knees, and learns to punch the ball from this position. Start by serving the ball into the goalkeeper from 4-5 metres away; ask them to train using both hands together to punch the ball. It is essential to keep the surface as flat as possible (with the thumbs outside the fist, not tucked underneath), and to contact the ball where you can see it — directly in front of the goalkeepers' view. The goalkeeper progresses to the right-hand or left-hand punch when they are ready. Always punch for height first, and distance second.

Exercise 3: PUNCHING (Intermediate and Advanced Levels)

➤ With a cone in the middle of the penalty area, you will begin on the goal line and approach the marker. Before touching the cone, the ball is served in the air for you to box away and over the top of the server.

➤ Punch the ball with your right hand, then your left. Finally, use both hands together. There are times when it is useful to punch the ball away from an attacker who is challenging. Whatever you do, don't punch the attacker!

POINTS TO REMEMBER

1) Clear for height and distance and keep your elbows in towards your body;
2) Take off with one leg and drive forward with the other.

Exercise 4: CROSSING WITH AND WITHOUT PRESSURE (Intermediate and Advanced Levels)

➤ As a goalkeeper, you will receive crosses from a variety of positions. The goalkeeper coach or trainer will step in the way, block, push or prevent you from collecting the ball. The idea is for them to apply pressure on you while you're trying to collect the ball in a crowd.

➤ After you intercept the cross, begin a counter-attack by quickly throwing or punting the ball into one of three target areas.

POINTS TO REMEMBER

1) Take the ball at the highest point;

2) Always secure the ball in your chest as quickly as possible; and look forward as soon as you regain your balance to initiate the counterattack;

3) Protect yourself with your knee facing the opposition.

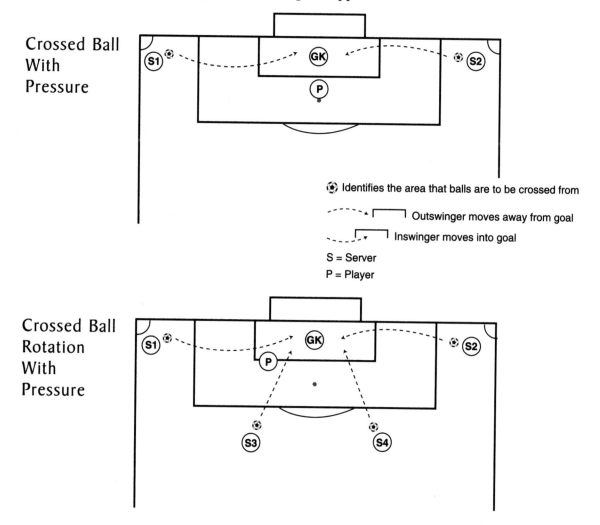

Crossed Ball With Pressure

Crossed Ball Rotation With Pressure

Identifies the area that balls are to be crossed from

Outswinger moves away from goal

Inswinger moves into goal

S = Server

P = Player

Exercise 5: CROSSED BALL AND SHOT ROTATION (Intermediate and Advanced)

➤ You will receive a cross from the right, with or without pressure, followed by a second cross from the left. Any ball not collected will stay in play. Then face a direct shot from the top of the penalty area and repeat the cycle.

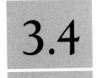

3.4 Counterattack

The goalkeeper is the last line of defence and the first line of attack. Learn to be aggressive on the counterattack.

FIRST, use the six-second rule and the element of surprise. When the time is right, take the ball to the top of the penalty area as quickly as possible and get ready to kick or throw the ball. Play the ball, otherwise keep it and look for an open player on your team.

SECOND, notice the position of the attackers. If most of them are in your zone, send the ball to a player on your team who can break into their half when they're not ready.

THIRD, always try to think two steps ahead — as you are about to receive or intercept the ball look up to see where your teammates are positioned. This helps you make a better decision and speeds up the counterattack.

FOURTH, the most dangerous ball is played long, creating a one-on-one situation toward the opponent's goal. There is also the chance that your team may be able to win the ball or knock down and attack from a favourable position on the field.

Exercise 6: CROSSING ROTATION
(Intermediate and Advanced)

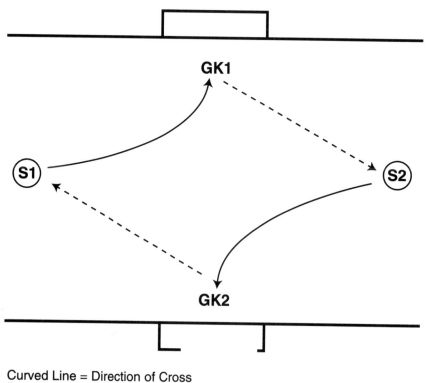

Curved Line = Direction of Cross
Dotted Line   = Direction of Throw

➤ Set two goals 20 metres apart with a goalkeeper in each and a server for each
goalkeeper. Servers cross balls to the goalkeepers, who must get the ball and send it
to the feet of the opposite server. Additional players should apply pressure to you as
the cross goes toward your goal.

➤ Next, goalkeepers play a one-on-one after receiving a ball crossed into the box. They
will put the ball to the ground and try to dribble around the opposing goalkeeper
before scoring.

Note: Goalkeepers should close down the space in front of the attacker.

Ian Bridge

Ian Bridge isn't a goalkeeper, but he's worked with plenty of them as both a defender and coach. One of his teammates was Canadian national team and English Premier League veteran netminder Craig Forrest. "He made me look like a great defender," Ian says. "Thanks Craig!"

Ian played professionally in the North American Soccer League, Canadian Soccer League and Swiss National League. Some of his favourite moments came with Canada's national team when it went to the World Cup in Mexico for the first time in 1986. He is the Canadian Under-19 Women's National team head coach (which won the silver medal in the inaugural FIFA World Championship) and is an assistant with Canada's National Women's team.

On the relationship between the goalkeeper and the defenders:

It is one of the most important factors in a successful backline. I define the backline as the back three, four or five, plus the goalkeeper. Keys to the relationship are: communication, trust, and positioning.

Good goalkeeping helps make better defenders:

The most encouraging thing for a defender is to know that you have a competent and confident goalkeeper behind you that will save all but the most difficult or precise shots on goal. Knowing this, you can always defend with confidence, allowing your opponent long range shots or shots from wide, low percentage positions while still being in a balanced position to tackle or dispossess the attacker when they attempt to get by you to the inside or into more dangerous space.

Conversely, if a defender is not confident in a goalkeeper's ability they will be anxious to stop or block all shots. This over-aggressive or over-eager attitude will enable a good attacking player to beat defenders and advance into more dangerous scoring positions.

Positioning and support is key:

Beyond the ability of a goalkeeper to help the backline in terms of confidence, a goalkeeper's positioning and support to the backline is of vital importance. For a defender, knowing that your goalkeeper is in the correct position to come for a cross ball or smother a penetrating pass will allow you to be "twice the defender you are alone." A high, active, supporting, dynamic goalkeeper will also save defenders from making long runs back toward the goal to clear or defend long passes played in behind the backline. This economical approach will allow the entire backline to remain focused and less fatigued — especially important at the end of games, when a high percentage of goals are often scored.

Ian Bridge at the FIFA U-19 Women's World Championship.
— Photo © Michael Stahlschmidt

What coaches can do to improve the relationship:

Coaches should try to train the backline (defenders and goalkeepers) as often as possible in game-like situations to improve their decision-making, technique and cooperation. "Good offense wins games. Good defense wins championships." Ultimately, the relationship between the goalkeepers and defenders is of great importance to a team's defense. I would much rather have a backline of organized, efficient players making most defensive plays look routine, than a backline that is constantly making life or death tackles or saves. The former is a group that works together and trusts each other. The latter is a group of individuals working alone that will be exposed or beaten by better attacking players.

Ian Bridge, Shel Brødsgaard and Lewis Page, on the sidelines at the FIFA U-19 Women's World Championship. — Photo © Dale MacMillan

Robert Douglas in action for Celtic in the Scottish Premier League.

— Photo © Dale MacMillan

On the Spot and In the Mind

The difference between stumbling blocks and stepping stones is how you use them.

— Anonymous

INTRODUCTION

I used to take pride in the accuracy and skill of my penalty shots as a young goalkeeper. When I was 16, I rigged penalty shot competitions with the other goalkeeper on our provincial all-star team, because I wanted so badly to be able to score from the spot in a game. I thought my impression in training would be able to influence the coach's decision. I certainly learned my lesson in many ways, over many years.

The first lesson came during the 1992 Canada West semi-final. I was in goal for the University of Victoria Vikings against the University of British Columbia Thunderbirds. I failed to score the seventh and deciding shot in the tiebreaker and our team was eliminated from the Canadian university championships. From that moment forward, I was determined not to be distracted during the penalty shoot-out and to focus solely on keeping the ball out of the net.

Coincidentally, I was in another penalty shoot-out the following season. Our team was facing an opponent from a very small town, one in which the entire community turned out to watch the game. It was the fifth shot for the opposition. All they had to do was score and the win would be theirs. The fans surrounded the penalty area and began to sing "Na, Na, Na, Na, Hey, Hey, Hey, Good-bye" before the player struck the ball. I read the shot, dove and extended myself fully to the right. It was my third save in five shots. I stopped the ball. And the singing, too. And, yes, our team went on to qualify for the next round of cup play.

4.1 Positioning

Before we go in-depth on penalty shots, let's consider proper positioning and angles. Being at the right place at the right time is the difference between making a save and watching the ball go into the net.

Proper positioning is a challenge for all who play soccer. To understand a safe distance from the goal line, make an imaginary line from the middle of the goal to the ball. Place yourself on the line in a position you feel comfortable to approach attackers or shooters.

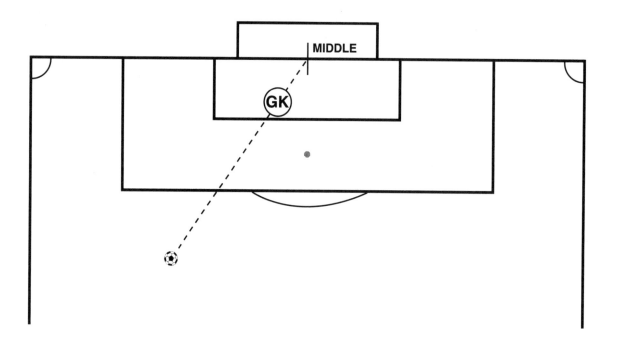

PROVIDING DEPTH IN THE GOALMOUTH

Positioning with
High Defensive
Pressure.

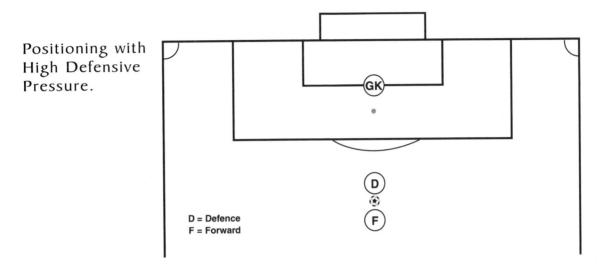

➤ It's important to provide depth in your position. In the first situation, a goalkeeper faces a shooter on or near the penalty area. If the player is under high pressure from a defender, you can safely close down on the shooter by stepping out to narrow the angle.

Positioning
with Low
Defensive
Pressure.

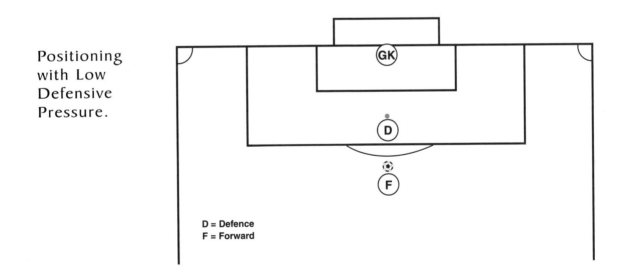

➤ In the second shooting situation, with low defensive pressure, you must change the position and stay on or near the goal line. That will give more time to react and make it easier to side-step the ball before making the save.

THE GOALKEEPER'S FOCUS ON ATTENTION

Focus your attention on situations you can control and ignore those that are less important or beyond your control. Concentration is a habit, not a talent. It needs constant practise.

Stay totally focused if the action is in your half. It's your job to help your team. On the other hand, if action is away from you, be ready to give support. In that case, you may relax from total concentration.

There are three zones on the field:
➤ the attacking third;
➤ the neutral third;
➤ the defensive third.

Recover your energy when the ball is away from you in the attacking third, but be ready to give support if needed. When the ball is in the neutral third, in midfield, begin to focus on the play and be ready for it to quickly come at you. When the ball enters the defensive third, be totally focussed. Nothing should distract you.

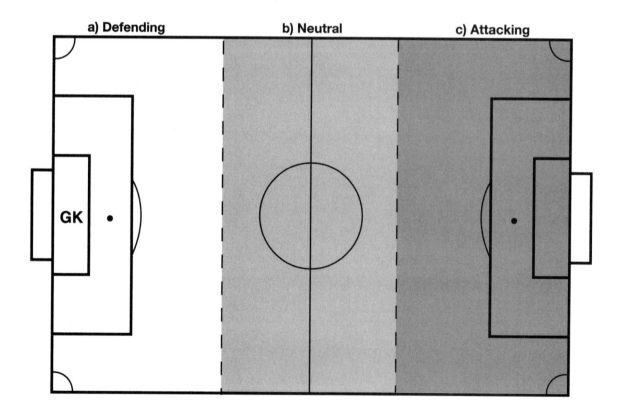

THE THIRDS RULE

Where is the best place for a youth goalkeeper to be when the ball is away from the goal area? A goalkeeper can and should be the first line of attack. Generally goalkeepers move away from the goal, towards the play at the opposite end of the field. You must also be able to move back, and change your position as the opponent proceeds down field with the ball.

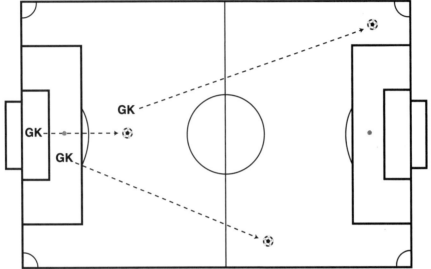

➤ Stay active to keep the correct angle from the goal wherever the ball is on the field. With practise and experience, you should know your position will be based on thirds, just like the rest of the field: the goal line to the goalkeeper's box; the goalkeeper's box to the penalty spot; the penalty spot to the arc of the penalty area. Stay busy during the game, moving in and out of your thirds.

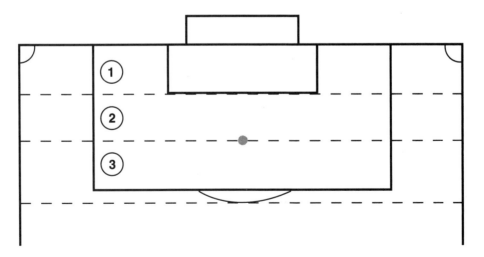

4.2 Communication

Like any other skill on the soccer field, communication must become a habit, through talking or using hand signals. Stay involved in the play by communicating with your team. Organize the backline when under pressure by the opposition. Provide information to the defenders in all situations with loud, early, clear and distinct calls. As a goalkeeper who communicates you stay in the game longer mentally because you are always watching the play.

On defensive free kicks, the goalkeeper must align the defenders with the opposition. Arrange the defensive wall with hand signals. Wave your arms to direct the players when they're lining up the wall to protect the near post.

Shout "keeper!" for every ball that you want. This will alert your teammates, who must cover the space behind you when you strive for the ball. It also helps intimidate the opposition. You can influence your opponent by actions and words.

4.3 Set Plays

Set plays are when play resumes after the ball goes out of bounds or a player is fouled. The most dangerous ones you'll face involve fouls committed by you or your team while defending against attackers. First and foremost is the penalty shot.

PENALTY SHOTS

It's a common mistake to guess where a player is going to shoot and then dive too soon. Consider the following tips to help increase the number of ways to save a penalty shot.

Stand your ground and rely on your reactions to make the save, rather than trying to guess by diving before the shooter makes contact with the ball. International stars, such as Mia Hamm or David Beckham, are capable of placing the ball into the most precise spot in the goal, which forces an international-level goalkeeper to guess where the player will direct the ball before it's kicked. These high-level goalkeepers prepare by reading newspapers or scouting reports and watching TV or videotapes to find out where shooters like to place a ball.

Do not allow the opposition to gain the advantage by showing your disappointment.

Obviously, the experience of an international goalkeeper will be different from that of the youth goalkeeper. You're facing youth soccer players who have less skill and accuracy. This method places the pressure on the kicker to beat you with a well-placed shot. You can increase the chance of saving the ball by making yourself as big as possible, standing your ground and reacting to the shot.

➤ To increase the likelihood of deflecting the ball after you dive, stretch and use any part of your body — even a tip of a toe or finger, to make the save. Use all of your attention to focus on keeping the ball out of the goal.

➤ In a game, do not argue with the referee or assistants about their decisions. Accept the calls, whether you agree or disagree. Focus all of your attention on the task at hand. Prepare to face the shooter. You cannot afford to waste time or energy by arguing with the official.

➤ Make eye contact with the shooter and don't look away. Watch the way a player lines up to take the shot and places the ball. Identify which foot they will likely use and pay attention to the player's angle of approach. Ignore the crowd. Your attention must flow smoothly; you should feel relaxed, confident and comfortable.

➤ Stare at the shooter with a smile on your face. Be confident and hide your nervousness. You may be able to read where the ball is likely to be placed in relation to the starting position of the shooter. Study the approach of the shooter and read the placement of their hips as they strike the ball toward goal. Saving a penalty kick is an unbelievable feeling — but do not overcelebrate, because the game's not over until the final whistle.

➤ Practise! Practise! Practise! Face shooters as often as possible who kick with their right and left foot in training. Remember, repetition is the key to success and make sure to have fun!

➤ In the event of a penalty shoot-out, do not take a penalty shot unless it is absolutely necessary for the goalkeeper to strike the ball. This will just take away from your level of concentration when you're needed most on your goal line.

Notes for the Shooter

SHEL'S TOP THREE TIPS FOR SCORING ON A PENALTY SHOT

1) Decide where you are shooting before taking a shot.
(Do not change your mind.)

2) Strike the ball low and hard to a corner.

3) Don't be fancy.

SETTING A WALL FOR FREE KICKS

Canadian National Women's team goalkeeper Nicci Wright says a free kick is almost as dangerous as a penalty kick. The difference is you can build a barrier by arranging teammates to distract the shooter and block the shot. Here are her tips for building a wall.

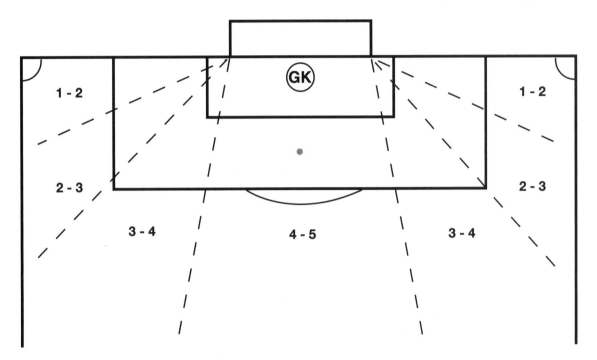

➤ The number of players you decide to put in your wall depends on where the free kick is from and the distance to the net. As a general rule, use a "1, 2, 3, 4, and 5" system for anything just outside the penalty area, up to about 20 metres out. This can vary, depending on age and skill level. Place one person for shots and crosses from the endlines of the penalty area, two for the middle-sides, three for the top corners, four for the left or right top portion and five for anything on the top that directly faces the net. If there is a free kick inside the penalty area, use anywhere from six-to-eight players — sometimes every player — depending how close the free kick is to the net.

➤ Lining up the wall depends on which side the ball is going to be kicked from. For free kicks from the right or left sides of the penalty area, always have the first person on the outside of the wall turn and face you to set up the wall. Sometimes one of the strikers will be identified before the game to set-up the wall. Make sure the outside shoulder of the second player in the wall is lined up with the post and the ball so

Four Person Wall

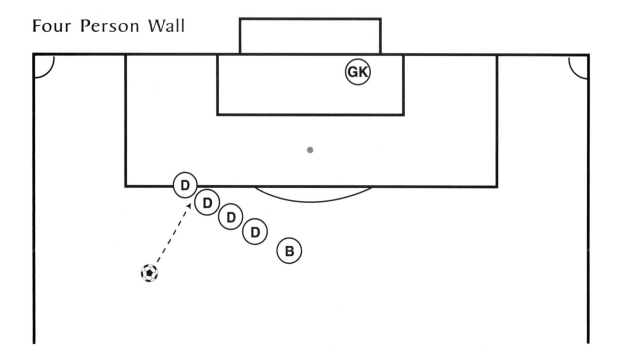

that when they turn around, there is a full body lined up outside the post so that any shot will go wide and end up either a goal kick or corner kick. Everyone else lines up next to the first person in the wall, towards the middle of the net. That way, you can move slightly to the other side of the net to cover any shots. Have the wall cover one side of the net, and you cover the other, but always be ready for a shot over the wall. You should be in a position to see the ball at all times!

➤ For any shots directly down the middle, line up the wall depending on the shooter. Some players may take free kicks from their strong foot, so set up the wall to force the kicker to use their weak foot. Although, some players can kick with either foot, so always be ready!

➤ Set up your wall quickly. All players should know if they are in the wall or not, because opposing players won't wait for you to set up your wall, they'll just shoot. Be quick and always have your eyes on the ball!

TIP: Decide before the game in a team meeting who can set-up the wall for the goalkeeper, who is going to be in the wall, and who is going to be the bullet. The bullet person charges the ball as soon as it has been put into play!

DEFENSIVE CORNER KICKS

It's very important for the defenders to cover the space left behind when you leave your goal to challenge for a crossed ball. It's also essential for you to communicate with the back line plus recognize the location of the opponent when decision-making in the goalkeeper's box. Always leave the line with confidence and determination.

*Note: This shows the **incorrect** stance, as the goalkeeper can't easily see what's behind her.*

Defending a Long-Range Free Kick

DEFENSIVE FREE KICKS

➤ Relay information to the back line and midfield when the opposition has a goal-scoring chance created by a free kick. Dangerous situations are nearest to the goal, especially towards the middle of the park. For example, there is more time to react when the ball is kicked in from the sidelines, because the farther away from the centre of the field, the greater amount of time the ball will spend in the air.

➤ The distance away from the goal is also important for you to consider. Identify the angle at which the ball will be struck toward goal: will it swing in or swing out? Establish a line for defenders to hold and close down the space behind them.

➤ Communicate your decision to attack the ball to the defenders so they can cover the space you leave behind.

➤ Make sure your defenders recognize who the opposition target will be and mark them accordingly.

4.4   Mental Training

Once upon a time there was a Danish goalkeeper named Henry From who made a spectacular save on a penalty shot in the semi-final at the 1960 Rome Olympics. Denmark was leading 2-1 against heavily-favoured Hungary and was under constant pressure. A penalty shot was called and the player to take the shot had not missed in 32 shots for his country. He was successful on 122 penalty shots in his career.

Henry, just before the shot was taken, walked over to his right post and stuck his gum on it. He made sure that the shooter noticed this. The shot was taken and Henry From made a diving save to the right-hand side of the goal. Denmark won the game, but lost in the final. A great result, nonetheless, for a small country. Thanks, in part, to From and a small piece of gum.

When he was interviewed later, From said he did not know where the shooter would place the ball, but he hoped that he would cause him to think about his shot. If he normally would shoot to the goalkeeper's right, then he would think that the goalkeeper knew this. And if he normally shot to the other side, then he would think that the goalkeeper knew this and would not have to worry about the right side. All he hoped was to make the player increase the pressure on himself. Some saves are never forgotten.

The journey towards goalkeeping excellence involves training to meet the physical, technical and mental demands of the game. One way is to create rituals, like kicking a goalpost before a penalty shot to find the correct frame of mind before facing the shooter. Or, creating checkpoints during the game at 20-minute intervals to re-focus and stay involved with the game.

Stay aware at all times. You may not be involved in the play for extended periods of time. Get in the habit of identifying three elements to focus on during the game or training session and stay focused on these topics for the duration. For instance, distribution, communication and crossed balls. This will help you stay concentrated. As they say, habits save the goalkeeper in pressure situations.

Another method for you as a teenage goalkeeper is to keep a journal based on your playing habits. This will help you judge the strengths and weaknesses of your performance, and to come to terms with attitudes and feelings rather than simply listening to the coaches or parents. By keeping a journal, you'll be aware of the areas in your game that give you the most confidence and those other areas that cause negative thoughts.

Finding a quiet place to close your eyes and think of playing a game is another method. It's called visualization. Apply key words or phrases to your imagination as cues to help regain control during the flow of play.

Communication is perhaps the most important way to successfully arrange your defense. It also keeps your mind involved in the game. Never be afraid to speak to the defenders and tell them what you see from where you are. Give them encouragement. Make the other team believe you are confident, strong, and difficult to beat. How you move your body and the way that you handle the ball can make such an impression. Your entire team's confidence will improve.

A NOTE FOR PARENTS

Finally, parents and coaches must be aware of the effect of a negative attitude towards the goalkeeper. Trust is invaluable for any goalkeeper and the parent or coach must always support the child's efforts to play the position. Many young goalkeepers place expectations well beyond their means on themselves, such as trying to stop every goal, or failing to accept that lack of height or size is a part of life. Realize that these are growing pains and take steps so that these fears will not impede their development. Everybody grows and everybody gets scored on. Reassure the goalkeeper of the positive elements of their game and release the negative situations as learning experiences.

When I began playing soccer competitively at the age of four, my dad knew a guy who was coaching a team of players two years older than me. I played for this team, the Lansdowne Evening Optimists, until I was 12. That's when the physical difference between myself and the others became too great. It was during this time that one of the scariest moments for any parent occurred. I was very small for my age, fearless, courageous, but not very physical. One day, the ball was played into the penalty area by an attacker. I slid onto my side to retrieve the ball at the same time as the opposing striker. He collided into me, feet first, and knocked the wind out of me.

Imagine, seeing your eight-year-old lying completely still on the ground, holding the ball and wheezing for air. My mother threw her purse into the air and ran onto the field from the halfway line to rescue her son.

This same person, at 45 years of age, used to come to watch me play as a professional and would sit in the grandstands with the biggest smile on her face.

"That's my son in goal!" she would declare when I stepped onto the field. She has come a long way in 20 years!

Loren Lidin

Loren Lidin wanted to be a goalkeeper since she was a three-year-old playing hallway hockey (needless to say, her mom likes to see her playing soccer outdoors). Loren, who lives in Vancouver, has tasted success with her team as a Coastal Cup champion, silver medalist at the British Columbia championships and the MVP at the Simon Fraser University indoor tournament.

My favourite part of playing goal:
I like the pressure that goes with the position. I like the training that I go through, and getting dirty. I also like to try and make the save that I am not supposed to make. I have always guarded my own space and as a 'keeper I get to do that.

My most memorable moment:
Going with my team to Prince George for the Under-12 provincials and winning a silver medal. I like the specialized training and the 'keeper games we play. I like the high level of competition that playing soccer brings. I also like being in net and having shots coming at me.

Loren Liden

My most embarrassing moment:
My first game with a new team at the start of the last season, I had a breakfast I shouldn't have had and during my shooting warm up, I threw-up all over my penalty area. I still played and felt great. The other team was grossed out and kept shooting from outside as they didn't want to step in it.

My favourite training game:
It's 2 vs. 2. There are teams made up of two keepers per team and they play-off against each other in a series of elimination games to decide the winning team. I like this game because it's lots of fun and competitive and works on lots of aspects of goalkeeping.

What I do in training to prepare for the game situation:
I enjoy training with older age groups of either girls or boys because I like being one of the weakest in the group as this pushes me to improve quicker. To learn about the game I find games to watch where 'keepers I look up to are playing in as I like to see how they handle the same situations that I get into. I get specialized 'keeper training, and read instructional material to see different views.

What I do off the pitch to improve my skills:
I watch as much as I can and feel a big difference in my game this season because of it. My favourite keeper to watch is Nicci Wright, from Canada's national team. Just watching her has helped me so much. I also have watched Erin McLeod and like her high style of play. I like to watch Andrea Neil play midfield as well. She is so tough.

Words of advice:
Train hard, have lots of fun, expect to be the hardest worker on your team and always think positive. It really works!

Nic Stankov, Shel Brødsgaard, Geoffrey Ayi-Bonte and Raegyn Hall.

Putting It All Together

Young people need models, not critics.

— John Wooden

INTRODUCTION

I have to admit, there is a major benefit to having a father who was a goalkeeper. He was always there to help, whether he was giving advice, training or introducing me to other role models. The two of us spent countless hours together, playing soccer or watching games in-person or on TV.

When I was 13, my team had a Provincial Cup game in Vancouver. That meant taking the ferry from my home on Vancouver Island. I passed time by playing video games in the arcade and eating a meal in the cafeteria. It was always difficult to sit still, especially being confined to the boat. There's not much space to kick a ball around!

The day before the final game, I practiced over and over with my father, handling balls he dropkicked from six to eight metres away. He would hit the balls hard and I would catch and hold them. Before each game, my dad would warm me up with exactly the same drill. I would enter a mental space that gave me the confidence to deal with all of the pressure.

During the game, when we had a one-goal lead, the ball was crossed directly to the feet of an opponent, six metres away. He volleyed the ball hard, right at me. I had my hands ready, caught the volley and held the ball.

The fans were shocked that I had stopped and held such a hard shot. After the game they could not stop talking about this amazing save. Fortunately, they had not seen my training on the previous day or my warm-up. Then they would have known that the shot was no different from what I faced in practice.

To this day, I regularly challenge Canadian national women's team goalkeepers Nicci Wright, Karina LeBlanc and Erin McLeod with volleys or dropkicks from the penalty spot. They get angry when I blast the ball past them, but we always laugh about it in the end.

5.1 Training Games for Goalkeepers

Put the skills you've learned in the first four chapters together and have a little fun with your teammates.

King Louis

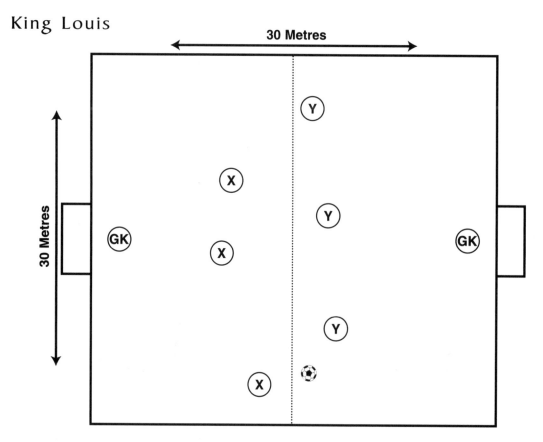

➤ Separate goalkeepers into two teams, one in each half of a 30-metre by 30-metre square. Work with your teammates to set-up each other on offence, strike the ball toward goal and block the ball on defence. Each time your team has the ball, take no more than three touches to shoot at your opponent's goal. The first team to 10 points wins.

➤ Keep the ball rolling. When it stops, possession changes to the other team. You may also try throwing or volleying the ball to pass and score. This will test your ball distribution skills.

GOALKEEPER MURDER

➤ This game is more fun than it sounds! It's played in a 10-metre by 10-metre grid with one ball between two players. One player begins as the attacker. The second player begins as the goalkeeper, who must dive at the opponent's feet to win the ball. The game begins with the attacker trying to dribble the ball past the goalkeeper. A point is scored by stopping the ball on the line — or within one metre.

➤ If the goalkeeper wins the ball by challenging the attacker, the roles are reversed and the game continues. When the ball crosses the sideline, the game restarts from where the ball left the field. Possession belongs to the player who did not kick the ball out of bounds.

➤ When the goalkeeper gains possession of the ball, they place one hand on top of the ball in order to keep possession and to prevent the opponent from regaining possession. Before they become the attacker and take their hands off the ball, the new goalkeeper must be a metre away from the player. As soon as a hand is lifted from the ball, the game begins.

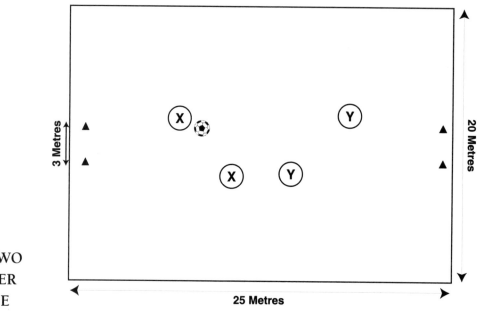

TWO-ON-TWO GOALKEEPER SCRIMMAGE

➤ This is just like Goalkeeper Murder, but with the playing space lengthened and three-metre goals placed at either end.

➤ Challenge the goalkeeper to demonstrate footwork skills. The game should last no more than five minutes, followed by one minute of rest.

BREAKAWAY GAME

➤ The object is for the goalkeeper to challenge the attacker in a one-on-one situation to win the ball by diving at the player's feet.

➤ Begin with 10 or so players dribbling the ball inside a 20- by 20-metre area. Simulate the game experience by asking them to take the ball at the goalkeeper, who must retrieve the ball and throw it outside of the area until each player has lost possession of the ball.

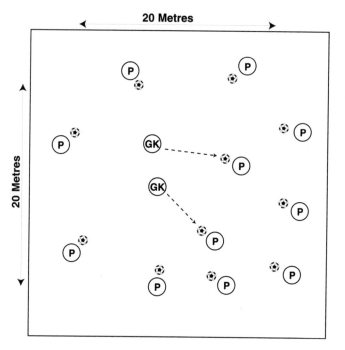

GOALKEEPER HANDBALL

➤ Divide players into two groups with one player in each goal on a 25-metre by 40-metre playing surface. Change the length and width of the field, according to the age and number of participants. Players pass or shoot with their hands or feet. The player with the ball is allowed to move two steps with the ball. All other players move freely into the available space. The defender guarding the player holding the ball will stay two steps away, preventing any unnecessary lunges or delays.

➤ The game may be modified in the following manners:
   1) One-armed throwing to shoot or pass;
   2) Volleys from the foot to shoot or pass;
   3) Double points for header goals;
   4) Open play.

GOALIE WARS

➤ Place one goalkeeper in each goal on a 15-metre by 20-metre playing area. The size of the goal will depend on the goalkeepers' ages. Points are scored by throwing or kicking the ball into the opponent's goal.

➤ When the goalkeeper makes the save and collects the ball, the game continues. When a goalkeeper blocks the ball and it rebounds into the playing area the opponent may rush to the ball, but then must dribble past the goalkeeper to score.

GOALKEEPER TENNIS

➤ Goalkeeper tennis, anyone? Divide a 12-metre by six-metre playing area in half with a rope. Place a goalkeeper in each half and have them catch the ball then volley the ball back into the opponent's court, over the top of the net.

➤ The game begins with the server who volleys the ball over the net into the opponent's area. A point is scored when the ball isn't successfully returned into the opposing playing area or when the ball hits the ground. First to reach 15 points wins.

NUMBERS GAME

➤ Place three or four goalkeepers in the centre of a goal, a step apart. Assign each goalkeeper a number. Before the server shoots towards the goal, a number must be called. The player whose number was announced has to react to the shot made from 10 metres away and make a save. All others must move to the side. Be concerned for the player at the end of the line and encourage the goalkeeper in this position to remain two to three steps off the goal line.

SHOOTING GALLERY

➤ The object of this game is to improve the goalkeeper's reaction time and deal with traffic in front of the goal. Begin the exercise with two teams, one shooting from across the top of the penalty area, and the other a group of goalkeepers spread out across the face of the goal.

➤ Each time the shot crosses the end line, whether inside or outside of the goal, the next player will strike toward the goal. Keep a running tally of the number of goals scored, switch the teams around and compete for the most goals to decide the winner.

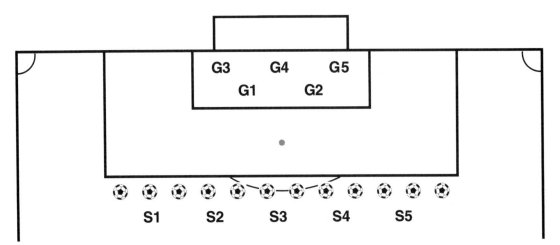

Jerry Knutsson

Jerry Knutsson is one of the world's most successful goalkeeper coaches. He's a coach with Fredrikstad in Norway's first division and was on Even Pellerud's coaching staff when Norway allowed just one goal in six games to win the 1995 Women's World Cup.

I met him in June 2000 when he joined the staff of Canada's National Women's team. Jerry's advice and guidance helped me become a better goalkeeper coach at the international level. It is a rare and unique privilege to meet a mentor.

Jerry says hard work and discipline are essential to success, but a goalkeeper trainer must be positive and encourage the goalkeeper at all times. Ultimately, only the goalkeeper can choose to be the best. It's entirely up to the athlete!

How do you build up a goalkeeper's confidence?
First, training equals repetition. When training a goalkeeper on a technique, such as crossed balls, allow them to handle hundreds of balls so they become confident in their abilities. Once they have mastered a technique, or skill, move on. There is always something to learn. If and when there is a recognizable weakness, focus on improving and learning to work on this area of the game. Finally, always encourage the goalkeeper to learn from their mistakes.

How do you become a better goalkeeper?
The best age to become a goalkeeper, if you're not one already, is between 14 and 16. If this is what you want to do, watch games on TV or live and study the strengths and weaknesses of all players to help yourself. Play with older players, the ball moves faster and quicker. Try other sports with similar body movements and associated tactical or technical demands, such as field hockey, European handball or basketball.

What is the best way for a goalkeeper to increase mental and physical strength?
In order to increase mental qualities, a goalkeeper must be prepared to work hard physically. You must set your own boundaries, which means 30 to 60 minutes per day, working on different parts of the body, in addition to team training. The exercises are not soccer-specific, but transferred from other sports. They must deal with muscle groups used by a goalkeeper. These activities can be done while you are relaxing or watching TV. Where a goalkeeper chooses this routine, they

develop and recognize that becoming an international level goalkeeper demands a unique and challenging lifestyle (four or five hours of training per day).

The goalkeeper needs to be fit enough to last beyond the duration of a 90-minute soccer game. Otherwise, the opposition gains an advantage. Physical commitment leads to mental strength and intensity. This can and will make a game easier. The stronger you are mentally, the higher level of intensity will be maintained.

What are the standards required for a goalkeeper to excel at the international level?

To excel at the highest level, you'll need to move fast over 10 metres and make decisions just as quickly. A strong level of physical fitness is essential. Plus, you need to develop the skill of reading the game, such as recognizing attacking patterns of play from the opponent and being involved with and/or interacting with your defense.

What is the role of a goalkeeper trainer?

Goalkeeper trainers are there to assess and recognize the strengths and weaknesses. Once a goalkeeper is conscious of these abilities, we must encourage them to make lifestyle choices to help them succeed. Only if, and when, they choose for themselves, must they make decisions to pursue this goal and suffer the consequences. Which means anytime family or friends take a holiday, or celebrate a birthday, the committed athlete will work around these distractions and remain focused on their goal to become the best.

Even Pellerud

Even Pellerud has made soccer his life. He played professionally in Norway for many years before serving as head coach of the Norwegian Women's National team, where he won Olympic and European Cup medals, plus a gold medal at the 1995 Women's World Cup. He became head coach of Canada's Women's National team in 1999.

The changing nature of goalkeeping:

The demands on a goalkeeper are always changing. From being mainly ball stoppers a couple of decades ago, the daily challenges of playing goal have increased tremendously:

— the higher number of crossed balls puts increased emphasis on hand skills, athleticism and courage;

— the faster pace of games at the higher levels means that the last player must read the game faster and more accurately;

— the penetration focus employed by most teams means that goalkeepers need to stay more composed and closely linked to the back line;

— and the new rules (back passes to hands not allowed) demands better footskills, but also the ability to communicate more effectively with the defence.

Qualities needed for the position:

In principle, the tasks have changed from being a

Even Pellerud
— Photo © Michael Stahlschmidt

goal stopper to becoming a goal scoring opportunity denier! Today, a good goalkeeper:

— should be a strong, confident leader with the ability to communicate often, loudly and accurately – in that order;

— needs to work effectively with the defenders in front of them;

— needs to have the mental strength to bounce back from mistakes, and to act with confidence instead of frustration.

The importance of confidence:

There are lots of good goalies out there that lose their self confidence and start to hide under pressure. The defenders and all other teammates and staff will accept mistakes, but they still like to see the goalie keeping a confident and focussed outlook. All the skills in the world cannot replace a goalie that has this mental power to positively influence a team just by his or her presence.

A Special Message for Parents and Coaches

Please, don't bore your goalkeeper.

To be honest, I've never really aspired to be a coach and I certainly don't profess to be an expert on all the strategies of the game, despite playing soccer all my life. But, if there is certainty when it comes to coaching soccer, it's the importance of recognizing the training needs of the goalkeeper.

The importance of goalkeeper-specific training, especially within a normal training session, cannot be stressed enough. Nothing is worse as a goalkeeper than being told by a coach to "go warm-up on your own," or "we'll need you in twenty minutes."

Unfortunately, very few youth teams have the luxury of a goalkeeper coach. However, even to ask the assistant coach to spend a few minutes to focus on the needs of the goalkeeper goes a long way to understanding and respecting the needs of the goalkeeper.

If the coach isn't able to work one-on-one with a goalkeeper, then have the goalkeeper join with the rest of the players in the drills that are planned. Even if the practice plan does not include a goalkeeper in the goal, today's rule changes mean goalkeepers can never get enough touches on the ball with their feet. The key is interaction with the coaches and players. Just like all the other players, impressing his or her coach and teammates in game-like situations motivates the goalkeeper.

For me, there is nothing more boring than going through drills on your own or with the other goalkeeper. Get the goalkeeper involved. An involved goalkeeper is a motivated goalkeeper. And a motivated goalkeeper can go a long way towards helping any team succeed.

— Paul Dolan,
former goalkeeper, Canadian World Cup Team and Vancouver 86'ers

Always A Goalie

In my childhood everything I did revolved around the game of soccer. I used to end up diving in mud puddles during the recess break at elementary school, saving shots from anyone who tried. Many times I was told by my parents to remove my clothes on the front porch before entering the house and going straight to the bathtub.

I also played the sport of lacrosse. Guess which position? Goaltender. The pads were so big I could hardly move. What a great feeling it is, being able to guard the goal in any sport.

For me, there was never a moment I did not think or dream about the game of soccer. At every one of my father's soccer matches I would take to the goal at halftime to stop shots. I would mimic my favourite player or try something my father taught me. I came across so many invaluable role models. They gave me their time and energy unconditionally. I learned by watching and asking questions. I now realize these impressions laid a foundation for the success I would experience on the field, both as an athlete and a coach.

I find myself giving more time and gaining more wisdom now as a coach. Judging by the way things are going, I will likely be saving the ball when I am old and walking with a cane.

It's just something I love to do. The game has been good to me.

— *Shel Brødsgaard, 2003*

Shel (holding ball) with one of his first soccer teams,
Victoria's Lansdowne Evening Optimists.

Acknowledgements

Many people have provided support and guidance throughout my career as a goalkeeper and coach. Their passion, leadership, knowledge and wisdom provided me the strength and desire to design and implement educational tools for youth goalkeepers and community level coaches.

I hope the next generation of goalkeepers will learn to respect, trust and value the fundamentals and playing philosophy promoted by me through Island Keeper Clinic. This book wouldn't be possible without the assistance of the following individuals and organizations:

Kjeld and Kathy Brødsgaard, Alert Bay, Nelson and Denman Island soccer communities, Geoffrey Ayi-Bonte, Sian Bagshawe, John Barretta, Laslo Bastyovansky, Colin Bedwell, Erling Borgstrom, Ian Bridge, Mike Cleghorn, Brandon Curr, Grant Darley, Mark Daugherty, Paul Dolan, Fulton family, Karen Gillman, Guy's Autochek & Repair, Raegyn Hall, Frans Hoek, Jerry Knutsson, Olga Lorenson and family, Jason Lowe, Macey family, Jeff Maughn, Richard Moller Nielson, Lewis Page, Robert Pagliaro, Pedersen family, Even & Anne Pellerud, Jason Pires, Purple Pirates, Scott & Fraser Rankin, Gordon Reading, Bernie Sainsbury, Bedste and Joe Schmidt, Soccer Saturday "Nutmeg" Groupies, "The Stalmeister," Robert P. Stankov (AKA "Big Daddy Denman"), Paul Sturrock, Team Sales Vancouver Island, Nicci Wright, Ziemer Bros. and the rest of the Northern Californians. Finally, to the original Team Sales Goalkeeping Clinic (established 1982): "Hip-hip-hooray for Team Volvo!"

And finally, special thanks to Bob Machin for his editorial assistance, the contributing photographers Christopher Grabowski, Dale MacMillan, Tony Quinn, Michael Stahlschmidt, and Jason Stang, the Canadian Soccer Association for access to their photos, Sportstown for the location to shoot photos, as well as Amy Apps, Sian Bagshawe, Chris Jackson and Big Daddy Denman for their contributions.

Photoshoot Participants

Geoffrey Ayi-Bonte

Sian Bagshawe

Maria Demare

Raegyn Hall

Tyler Lewis

Loren Liden

Nic Stankov

For additional copies of the book *Soccer — Guarding the Goal*, contact your local bookstore, or www.guardingthegoal.com

An instructional video, *Guarding the Goal* is available for the community-level coach and youth goalkeeper, aged eight to seventeen. The cost is $34.95 (Canadian funds), plus applicable taxes, and postage.

Shel Brødsgaard is available to lead goalkeeper development programs for 'keepers and coaches in your community.

Please contact Island Keeper Clinic for any of these products at
270 Plowright Road,
Victoria, B.C. Canada V9B 1P3
E-mail: **islandkeeperclinic@hotmail.com**
Phone: 250-744-6041 or 604-240-1655
www.islandkeeperclinic.com

Brad Friedel, U.S.A. goalkeeper, celebrates during the FIFA 2002 World Cup.

— PHOTO © DALE MACMILLAN

PRACTICE PLANS

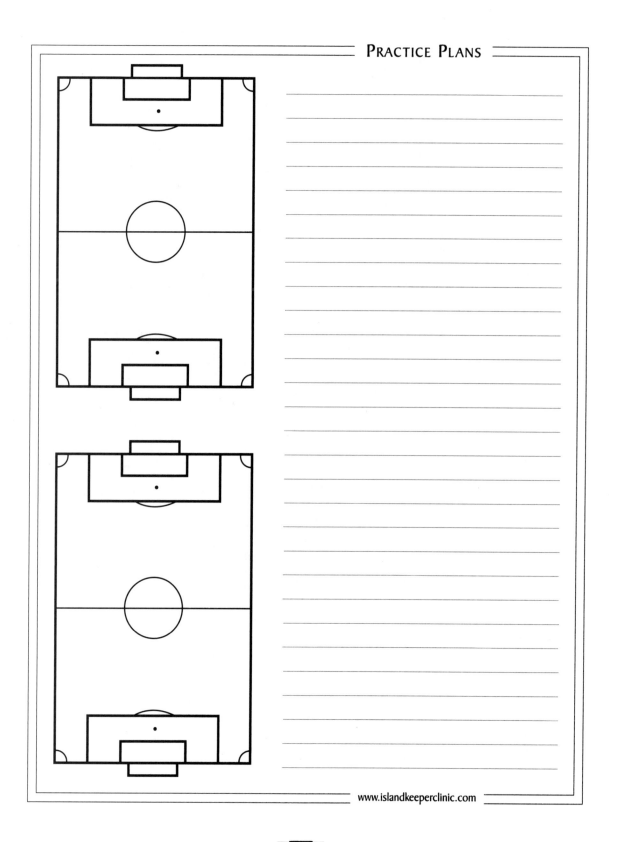

www.islandkeeperclinic.com

PRACTICE PLANS

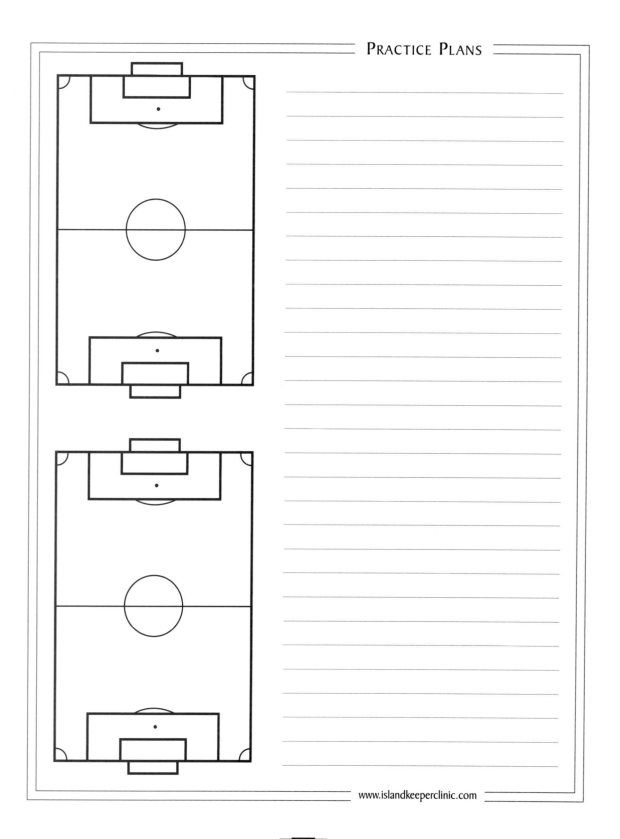

PRACTICE PLANS

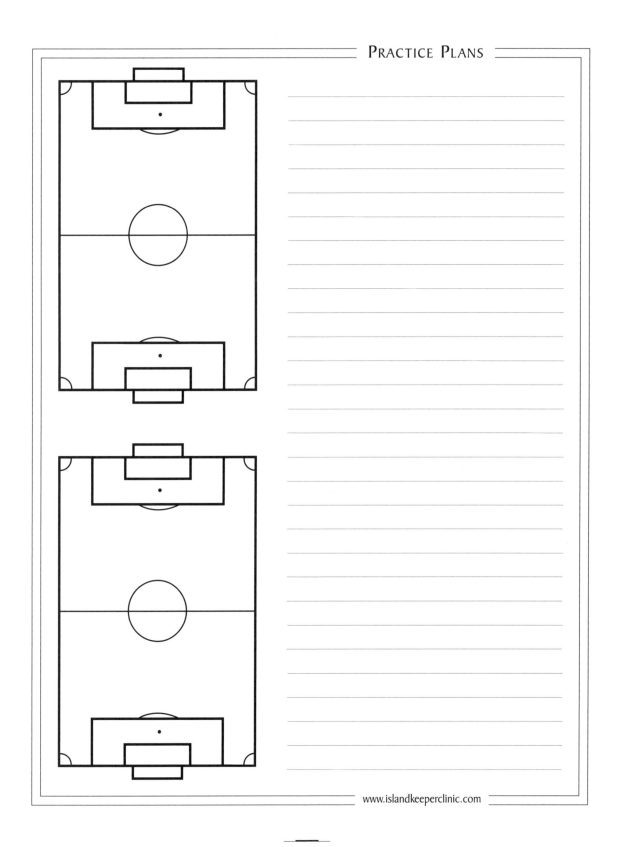

www.islandkeeperclinic.com

Practice Plans

Goalkeeper's Journal

Goalkeeper's Journal

Goalkeeper's Journal

Goalkeeper's Journal

Goalkeeper's Journal